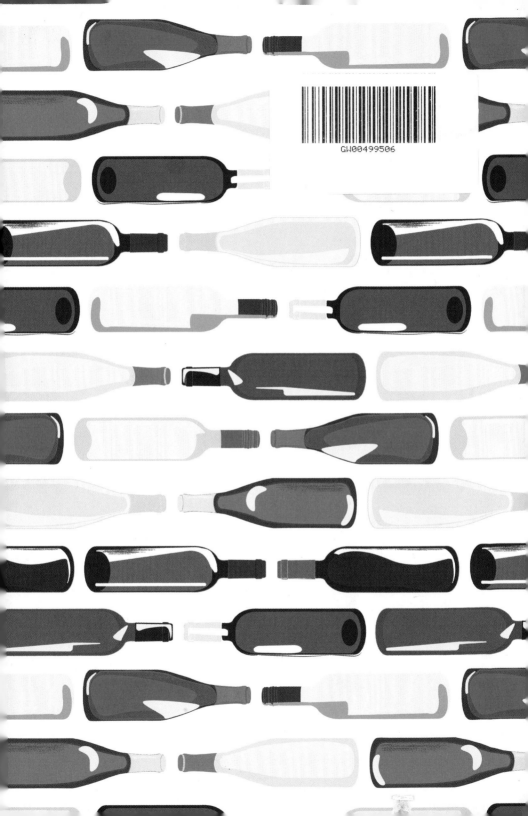

GW00499506

TEN

GRAPES

TO KNOW

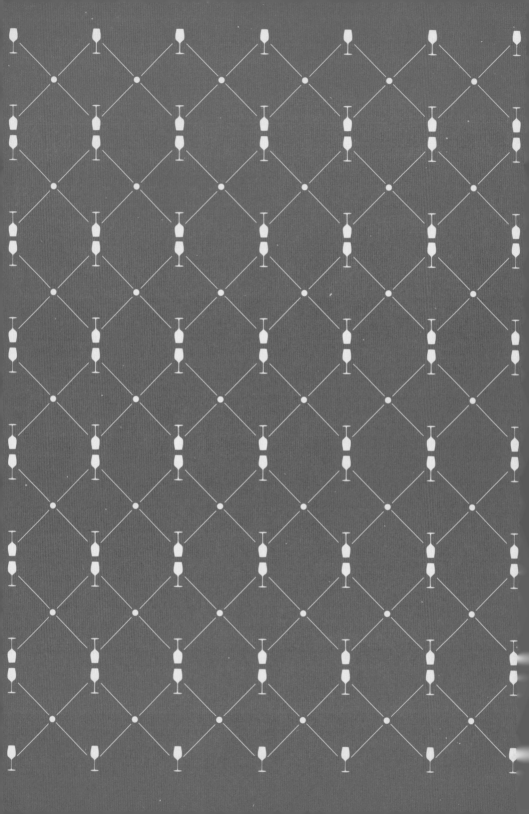

THE TEN & DONE WINE GUIDE

TEN GRAPES

TO KNOW

CATHERINE FALLIS

MASTER SOMMELIER

THE COUNTRYMAN PRESS

A division of W. W. Norton & Company

Independent Publishers Since 1923

Manufacturing by Versa Press
Book design by Anna Reich
Illustrations by Alyssa Roberts Comstock
Production manager: Devon Zahn

The Countryman Press
www.countrymanpress.com

A division of W. W. Norton & Company, Inc.
500 Fifth Avenue, New York, NY 10110
www.wwnorton.com

978-1-68268-253-1 (pbk.)

10 9 8 7 6 5 4 3 2 1

For Miles

CONTENTS

Preface   8
Introduction   10

1. **PINOT GRIS/GRIGIO**   33
2. **SAUVIGNON BLANC**   47
3. **CHARDONNAY**   61
4. **VIOGNIER**   77
5. **PINOT NOIR**   89
6. **SANGIOVESE**   111
7. **SYRAH/SHIRAZ**   127
8. **MERLOT**   141
9. **CABERNET SAUVIGNON**   153
10. **ZINFANDEL**   169

Acknowledgments   184
Check Your Success Quiz Answers   185
Resources   186
Index   187

PREFACE

Every time I shop, I observe folks standing in the wine aisle, struggling over which bottle to choose. I eavesdrop on their cell phone conversations. They go something like this:

> *"Hi. I'm at the market. Which Chardonnay should I get? The one with the critter on it is on sale, but it's not very good. The one we usually get is thirty dollars but I would like to stay under twenty. What should I try?"*

In a restaurant, there is at least a server, bartender, or perhaps even a sommelier to help navigate the selections. But are they genuinely trying to help you or just build up the check or make a commission? Trust is an issue and it becomes a bigger deal when you are considering a $100 bottle on a menu versus a $15 bottle on the shelf.

I wrote this book to illustrate that with just a little investment of time, and with a focus on ten essential grapes and the wines they make, you can become sufficiently well versed to navigate most wine situations with confidence and ease. I spend most of my time teaching, training, certifying, and adjudicating exams at a very high technical level. I even write technical works for that audience. This is not one of them. I am putting you in the driver's seat. Take a spin through these chapters: Pinot Gris/Grigio, Sauvignon Blanc, Chardonnay, Viognier, Pinot Noir, Sangiovese, Syrah/Shiraz, Merlot, Cabernet Sauvignon, and

Zinfandel. Check out a chapter with a grape you already know, or read them in order. It's up to you!

In my journey to becoming a Master Sommelier, so much of the information was presented in a manner that was not only mindboggling in its scope, but also made me feel like an outsider, not a member of the secret society. I found it terribly intimidating and snobbish. I still do, from time to time. Over the years I have developed a reputation, aided by my first boss in the biz, Kevin Zraly, and my experience backpacking around Europe in my early twenties, of simplifying complicated materials and making the presentations and material straightforward, concise, and not at all technical when writing for or presenting to consumers. I named my company Planet Grape, and my alter ego, grape goddess. While I am a highly credentialed expert and you can trust in the information I provide, I want to make wine inviting, down-to-earth, and fun.

Let's start with the basics of tasting, pairing, shopping for wine, and ordering wine in restaurants. If you'd like to delve into the information here, feel free. If you'd like to skip right to one of the grapes, go for it. In each chapter, I share the history of the grape, where it is grown, it's taste profile and the styles of wine produced from it, dozens of specific wines to try, anecdotes from my career in wine, and more. Either way, most of your basic wine questions are answered here, and this will serve as a useful reference tool. Enjoy!

INTRODUCTION

Wine, like food, is a pleasure for the senses. We use our eyes, our nose, and our palate as often as we eat. Enjoying a glass of wine requires the exact same tools—nothing more, nothing less.

How do we enjoy wine? Let me count the ways. Just as in food tasting, or eating, we use our senses of sight, smell, and taste. Occasionally our ears receive anticipatory pleasure messages—the sound of popcorn popping, or the pop of a Champagne cork. We also use our sense of touch, as in the sheer sensual pleasure in a bite of silky, creamy chocolate pudding, or in a glass of buttery Chardonnay.

We've been given a complimentary toolbox! We all have the senses, if we are lucky, of sight to enjoy a wine's beauty, of smell to enjoy its perfume, and of a palate to taste and feel a wine. Our preferences are unique, and fully our own. These preferences apply to coffee—whether you like it strong, black, and bitter or frothy, creamy, and sweet—as they do to wine. You like what you like, and you don't have to defend yourself! Our individual tastes, like our fingerprints, are as distinct, unique, and varied as the hundreds of thousands of vineyards around the world.

Looking to their origin, the best wines are from well-sited vineyards that have a natural capacity to produce superior raw material; in this case, grapes. Winemakers work with these top-quality grapes but the best of their lot will give credit where credit is due: to Mother Nature.

Historically, the fine wine-producing countries of the world have had the right soil and favorable weather conditions, and have looked at wine production and consumption as an important part of their history and culture. Grapes for wine production are generally grown at latitudes 30° to 50° north and south, and include two general groupings, Old World and New World.

Wines from the Old World include those from European countries, such as France, Italy, Spain, Portugal, Germany, Austria, Switzerland, and Hungary. Old World vineyards are generally situated in cool climates, where grapes struggle to ripen and their quality reflects annual weather patterns. Therefore, each vintage is unique and there is great variation from year to year. (The "vintage" is the year the grapes were harvested—if the grapes were picked in 2016, that means that wine's vintage is 2016.) The premium wines of the Old World also tend to reflect more of the character of their origin, a distinct personality, rather than just offer-

ing straightforward fruit characters. These wines are typically identified by their region of origin and in most cases do not have grape names on the label.

Exuberantly fruity wines generally come from warmer New World climates, from regions that include North and South America, Australia, New Zealand, and South Africa. Dependable sunshine gives more reliable quality year after year, but individuality is sometimes hard to find in these wines. In the United States and other New World wine regions, wines tend to be named after the grape variety rather than the region of origin.

This theme of Old vs. New World will play itself out with the grapes covered here, so it will become more familiar as you move through the book.

Now for the fun part—tasting! For hedonistic enjoyment, sit back, relax, and enjoy the ride. For a deeper dive, and further education, sit up, see, swirl, sniff, taste, and jot down what you are experiencing.

GRAPES

Grapes, like wheat, corn, apples, and coffee beans, are an agricultural crop cared for by farmers. With the cooperation of nature, some of these crops result in raw material so amazing it will take your breath away. The best

> Jelly Bellies come in dozens of flavors from jalapeño to root beer, but, in the end, they're all jellybeans. Grapes, too, come in dozens of varieties from Chardonnay to Zinfandel, but in the end, they're all grapes!

raw material usually manifests itself into the highest-quality products. *Vitis vinifera*, the grape species native to Europe and Central Asia, is responsible for 99.99 percent of the world's quality wine production. Nearly all wine consumed in the world is from *Vitis vinifera*.

If you understand apples (or Jelly Bellies), you understand wine grape varieties. Chardonnay and Merlot are varieties of grapes, just as Granny Smith and Red Delicious are varieties of apples.

Wines are labeled with either their variety (or blended grape character) or their geographical origin. In France, wines are traditionally named after their region of origin. In the United States, wines are named after the variety. A white Burgundy from France and a California Chardonnay do have one thing in common—they are both made of Chardonnay! Red Burgundy is Pinot Noir.

SENSE EXERCISE

Apple Varieties

Go to the fruit section in your favorite market, and head to the apples. Count the number of apple varieties on display. You might find Golden Delicious, Granny Smith, and Fuji. What do they have in common? What are their differences? When you get home from the market, log on to your favorite search engine and check out the apple varieties you've noted. Does one have a softer texture? Which is the sweetest? The juiciest? Now, search for Chardonnay and see just what you come up with.

WINE

Wine is approximately 90 percent water. The rest is made up of color, aroma, flavor compounds, alcohol, acid, sugar, grape skin tannins, barrel tannins, and trace vitamins and minerals.

AROMA is the most important part of serious, focused wine tasting and professional evaluation. Using your nose is easy. Describing what you smell is where the challenge lies. Concentrate, forget the mind-boggling winespeak, and just say whatever comes to mind. Remember, it's your nose. Whatever you say is right!

Ninety percent of what we perceive as taste is smell, so the nose is key. Smells warn us of danger. Smell something once and you'll never forget it; this is an age-old defense mechanism. Smell is the most evocative sense; it is deeply connected with memory and emotions. Smell triggers the pituitary gland and controls moods. Smell can excite, relax, arouse, or make us romantic. Smell influences how you

Here is some nose trivia: it is the main organ used in tasting; professional tasters are called "noses"; smell is a direct route to your brain; and smell cells continually divide and grow, so you have a new "nose" every three weeks.

think, feel, and react. Sight and smell together can make your mouth water. Once it is watering, your tongue's sensory receptors get to work on processing the various sweet, salty, sour, bitter, and other flavor components. In nature, females, be they human or animal, tend to have a heightened sense of smell, believed to alert them to danger so that they may protect their offspring. It is possible to heighten sensory reception and focus by eliminating distractions.

What is a blind tasting? Blind tasting is simply a method of tasting where the wine in your glass is a complete mystery to you. A systematic, deductive process is used to help determine what the wine is. When approaching this task, think of yourself as Sherlock Holmes. Clues are everywhere, in the wine's appearance, aromas, on the palate, and on the finish, or aftertaste. You build your case based on these clues and come to a logical conclusion. Professionals taste wine blind so as to give impartial reviews. Snobs blind taste to impress their audience by nailing the wine's identity.

SENSE EXERCISE

Blind Cola Tasting

Get three types of soda pop, such as cola, cherry cola, and root beer. Have someone pour each one in a different glass, and set them in order: 1, 2, and 3. Close your eyes, hold your nose, and see whether you can taste the differences among the three.

BODY is the word used to describe how a wine feels in your mouth, its mouthfeel—its weight and fullness. *Body* refers to a combination of the wine's alcohol and sugar content.

As a rule of thumb, the less acid, and the more sugar and/or alcohol, the more viscous, or fat, or heavy the wine feels in your mouth. Many Chardonnays go through a process called malolactic conversion (wine geek alert!), in which their natural malic acid (think tart green apples) is converted to lactic acid (think heavy cream), and thus end up thicker and fuller-bodied than other white wines.

One of the world's most influential wine critics, Robert Parker, openly admits his preference for the "bigger is better" school. In his newsletter the *Wine Advocate*, he gave a high score to a particular French Sauternes, one of the most elegant, subtle, and discreet dessert wines in the world, because he found it "corpulent, full-bodied, unctuously textured, mouth-filling, well-endowed, and hefty."

ASTRINGENCE is a physical sensation that actually constricts the muscles on your palate when they come into contact with sour, bitter, or tart substances. This is one of the reasons astringent, or tart, wines do not win high scores from the wine press. They are tasted alone without food and are easily overshadowed by the bigger, beefier, fruitier, oakier, everything-er wines.

Wine has intrinsic tartness. This is one of the reasons it has graced tables for so many centuries: tartness serves to stimulate the gastric juices as well as to cleanse the palate between bites. But many of today's most highly rated wines are crafted to please the palate without the benefit of food. While enjoyable on their own as cocktails, unfortunately these 100-point blockbuster-style wines are unbalanced and generally unsuitable for the table.

TANNINS give a drying, chewy, or gripping quality that seems, at first, unpleasant. One form of wine tannins comes from skins, stems, and pips (seeds) of the grapes. The other form of wine tannins, wood tannins, derives from oak barrels, in which some wine is aged, and can leave your palate feeling as if you just chewed on a two-by-four if too aggressive, or simply add a sweet, vanilla bean, or toasty nuance. Tannins are most commonly encountered in dry red wines. This is why many people prefer white, or even blush wines, which are smooth, occasionally off-dry, and voluptuously round and soft. The chalky, grainy, sometimes bitter tannins, however, give a wine longevity—the ability to age—and, more important, provide a pleasant contrast to the richness of your meal. Think of an ice-cold glass of tea on a hot day; that little pucker is half the fun of it! Remember that tannins dry out your mouth, whereas acidity makes your mouth water.

Tannins from the grapes contain phenols, those healthful compounds thought to lower cholesterol and reduce the risk of cancer. Red wines, whose skin-contact time is longer during the winemaking process, tend to have more of the invigorating tannins. Luckily, their bitterness is balanced out with ripe fruit character. Over-steeped tea is not so bitter when you add sugar or cream. Drinking green tea, or eating chocolate or red grapes, especially the skins, are other ways to get those healthy phenols into your system.

SENSE EXERCISES

Astringence
Get a lemon and cut it into wedges. Bite into a wedge. Now, take that same lemon wedge and sprinkle it with sugar. Take another wedge and sprinkle it with salt. Taste both wedges. Do you notice that salt and sugar both lessen the lemon's astringency?

Tannins
Steep a regular tea bag in a cup of hot water as if you were preparing a cup of tea. Leave the bag in for one hour. Approach the cup slowly. Pick it up, take a small sip, swirl it around in your mouth, and then spit it out! You are now officially a tannin expert.

Tasting Wine
Buy a roll of assorted fruit-flavored Life Savers and a small notebook. Take out one of each flavored candy, setting them on a piece of white paper in front of you. Pick up the first one. Note its appearance, including color. Then smell it once and jot down a few descriptors that pop into your mind. Now put the Life Saver in your mouth, and again, without thinking, write down whatever words come into your head. Repeat this with each flavor in the pack. Now, take out another set of the candies and set them down in front of you in a random heap. Close your eyes. Pick one up. Smell it. Do you recognize it? Pop it into your mouth. Now you really are onto something. Is it cherry? Is it orange?

Congratulations. You are on your way into the world of wine tasting. While the variables are far greater than what is in a roll of Life Savers, the basic principles are the same.

Place a few different glasses of wine in front of you, and practice the same exercise as with the Life Savers. Note the colors, aromas, and tastes, taking notes in your logbook. Close your eyes and try to pick out which is which, and take note of what clues were the strongest to you. Perhaps a red wine you are tasting has a cherry flavor. Anytime you taste this cherry flavor from now on, make a note (mental or written) of what the wine is. Cherry could now be your "marker" for Pinot Noir, Sangiovese, or Merlot, for example.

This is more fun with a partner or small group, but remember to taste quietly and try not to be influenced by what the others are saying. Listen to your own impressions. They are the only sure thing.

FILLING YOUR DESCRIPTOR TOOLBOX

Wherever you are, begin paying attention to colors, aromas, and tastes. If passing by a florist or open-air market, smell a yellow rose and compare that mentally to the fragrance of a red rose. When near the sea, take in that fresh, briny smell. Go into a coffee roastery and stick your nose into the various bins of beans. At a natural foods market where spices and herbs are sold in bulk, open up and smell, smell, smell! At home, head to the spice rack and take a whiff of tarragon or cloves. In the kids' room smell crayons, or Play-Doh. In the bathroom, smell suntan lotion, Vicks VapoRub ointment, baby powder, body lotions, shampoos, soaps, perfumes, aftershaves, and colognes. Soon your mind will be overflowing with sensory adjectives. Having these many different descriptors at your disposal makes it so much easier to write down and also verbalize what you are smelling and tasting in wine.

The lexicon of wine is not all that different from a lexicon of music or semiconductors or sports or fashion. Any industry has its code—certain words that "civilians" wouldn't know. In the restaurant industry, for instance, a nonindustry person is a civilian. We can identify the civilians at a party and know not to automatically offer them shots of Fernet-Branca with a PBR chaser. Among ourselves, we can say something is 86'ed and understand it is sold out for the night. Wine reviews, marketing materials, and restaurant wine lists are saturated with words wine industry "civilians" wouldn't know. Words like *terpenes* or *batonnage*. I like to use more familiar language, as you will see in the shopping section for each grape, and I like to bring the wine to life by comparing it to a musician, or giving it a dating profile. An artist might paint a picture to capture the personality of the wine. The best thing you can do is to learn about the wines firsthand, then write down a few words describing it. For example, "This Viognier was like eating apricot tartlets in a flower shop."

In describing wine, you can also draw from the language of your world, whether that is fashion, graphic design, engineering, music, or art. For example, a music lover might say one wine is edgy and energetic like DNCE and another is mellow and comforting like Ed Sheeran.

As you build up your supply of markers, such as cherry and Pinot Noir, or butter and Chardonnay, you'll be building your own tasting memory that will last a lifetime. I can't stress enough: taking notes will help to jog the memory down the road. Besides fruit characters, such as cherry or apple, with practice and focus you will eventually start to register floral, spice, herb, mineral, vanilla, earth, or even medicinal aromas and flavors. Over time, you may notice a regional character streak, such as the difference between a Sauvignon Blanc from Napa Valley and one from France's Loire Valley.

Perfumes, aftershaves, fragranced hand and body lotions, and even some hair products provide enough distraction for the average nose to impair its ability to read what is in the glass. So do cooking or food smells. Wineglasses, by the way, should be completely odor-free to begin with. The only way to guarantee this is to wash them with hot water only. No soap. No bleach. Just water. Use Riedel brand glasses if you like (Riedel rhymes with "needle") but the $4 wineglasses at Crate and Barrel are equally impressive and comfortably priced. A small red wine glass works well across the wine spectrum, or if you prefer to branch out, look to a standard white wine glass, then both a globe-shaped larger stem for Chardonnay and Pinot Noir, and the less curvaceous but equally large-bowled "Bordeaux" glass for everything else. Feel free to add flutes for sparkling wine as well. Stemless glasses are fine and fit in the dishwasher. In general, thinner, lighter glass enhances the experience.

HOW TO TASTE

The best time to evaluate wines is first thing in the morning, before the senses are barraged. Hunger brings a heightened sensitivity and increases sensory perception.

Use your senses. Note your sheer, visceral reactions. Don't think. Just react. You can do it! Use this as a jumping-off point, to give your tasting some structure. Don't worry too much about the details. Jot down what you see, smell, and taste if words pop into your mind. This gets easier over time.

SEE

Look at the surface. Tilt the glass against a white background. Look at color, depth of color. Look at viscosity (thickness). Some wines move like fat-free milk, others like whole milk, and some even like cream.

SWIRL

Gently swirl the wine around in the glass to allow oxygen to get in the wine and help it open up and show its character. Practice this on a table or other surface. Ready to go mid-air? Wear dark colors just in case.

SMELL

Take a whiff, but don't inhale. Are any words coming to you? They will as you do this more often. It's like riding a bike. Once you've done it, you think to yourself, "What took me so long?" To get more serious, check out A. C. Noble's website The Wine Aroma Wheel. Just imagine working at an ice-cream shop all summer. Each day at work, you taste several flavors. By the end of summer, you could close your eyes and recognize most of the aromas and flavors and let out a steady stream of beautiful descriptors simply because you spent the last few months getting to know them. You have become an ice cream expert!

TASTE, GARGLE, AND FEEL IT

Moving the wine around your mouth is a great way to enhance your various sensory perceptions. First, take a very small bit of wine into your mouth. Then, purse your lips and gently draw in oxygen. Now, carefully move the wine around as if swishing with mouthwash. Warning: Practice this at home only. Gargling wine in public may lead to a quick exit by your dinner companion.

Now, let it rest. What are the sensations you are registering? Is it light or full? Dry or sweet? Flavors? General sensations? Do the flavors linger? This is called the finish, and the longer the finish, the higher the quality of the wine.

Did you like it? Did the wine deliver pleasure? Is the price right? If yes, then it is a good wine. Take it all in with a grain of salt, and remember, wine is totally and completely a personal experience.

SENSE EXERCISE

Finish

Buy a Baby Ruth, a PayDay, and a Hershey's bar. Unwrap them and set them on a piece of white paper. Take a bite, then jot down a few notes in your journal, using any words that come to mind. Repeat with each candy bar. Which one has the longest finish?

PAIRING

Wine, like food, is simply a part of the meal, a source of pleasure, and, if it is of good quality, a reflection of its origin. Wine is as easy to enjoy as food, but so often we get hung up on trying to use the right jargon, or to pair the wine with just the right dish. Relax. Take a deep breath. Stop thinking. And let your senses take over.

Sit back, close your eyes, and imagine taking a bite of a Big Mac, a burrito, or a big spoonful of macaroni and cheese. What is your reaction? Is your mouth watering? Good. You are now ready to begin.

How do we enjoy food? Just as in wine tasting, we use our senses of sight, smell, and taste. Occasionally, our ears send pleasure messages. Pick up a flute of Champagne and listen to the self-renewing stream of bubbles. We also use our sense of touch. Texture is a source of sheer sensual pleasure, especially when enhanced by positive flavor and aroma jolts. Take caviar, for example. Imagine those silky little globules sliding across your palate, only to be squeezed softly and popped, their briny contents oozing out and coating your tongue. Try to put your sensations into words. Now take a sip of wine, and put your sensations into words. How did you do? Repeat this exercise often.

Caviar is not for you? What about chocolate truffles? Just the sight of a truffle can bring a smile to the face of a chocolate lover. Pick one up and roll it gently between your fingers. Notice the dusting of cocoa powder on your fingers, which now you must lick off. But not, of course, until you have deposited the decadent morsel into your mouth. In it goes. Start to roll it around in your mouth. Is it sweet yet? No. It is silky from the cocoa powder. Bite into it, and finally arrive at the sweet, creamy, soft, and gooey core of chocolate. Say the words *silky*, *soft*, and *creamy* to yourself. Have you ever had a wine you'd describe this way? If not, try a sip of Chardonnay or Pinot Noir. Are you feeling it?

Slowing down helps focus our sensory receptors. Being hungry brings them into razor-sharp focus. This is something I learned while going through a series of wine-tasting exams. When was the last time your mouth was watering, really watering at the thought of what was to come? Anticipation is a good first step toward maximizing pleasure.

Sweetness, saltiness, textures, and richness are all components that add to sensual pleasure. So does earthiness, for some. Earthy vegetables, such as eggplant or mushrooms, and game, for example, take us someplace our ancestors have been. Add wine to the picture and you add another layer of pleasure. Some wines are earthy, and in combination with earthy foods can take you right to paradise. Some wines are sweet and silky; some are earthy and silky. Take France's Burgundy, for example. Red Burgundy, made from Pinot Noir, is earthy and silky. White Burgundy, made from Chardonnay, is earthy and unctuous. Good California Pinot Noirs and Chardonnays occasionally mimic these sensations, though most often with a fruitier slant.

Here's an example of ramping up sensory pleasure: macaroni and cheese, drizzled generously with truffle oil. Macaroni and cheese brings back pleasant childhood memories and is so satisfyingly creamy and tangy. Adding the silky, earthy oil is enough to drive anyone wild. Serve with a glass of white Burgundy and prepare for liftoff!

The old rules—white wine with fish, red wine with meat—have, for the most part, gone by the wayside. Newer rules include those explored in *Red Wine with Fish: The New Art of Matching Wine with Food*, by David Rosengarten and Joshua Wesson, originally published in 1989. This logical tome looks at elements in the dish: salty, acidic, sweet, and bitter; flavors: fruity, nutty, smoky, herbal, spicy, cheesy, earthy, and meaty; light vs. rich textures; and the wild cards wine has of tannins and alcohol. By the way, don't you feel smart? After reading through these chapters, you will be on familiar ground with all of these descriptors! Then there are those who want to throw away the rules, who say "drink what you like and eat what you like," though they agree that some sense of weight and balance is helpful. Not sure what to serve? Drink whatever you like, and serve whatever you think your guests will enjoy, whether they are royalty or gentlemen, rogues, peasants, or your in-laws. Remember, as with other facets of life, balance is the key to a good match.

If you think those sophisticated Europeans have some kind of ingrained wine knowledge, think again. The average person there knows about as much as we do—squat! So how do they know what wine to have with what dish? Easy. They follow centuries-old regionally based traditions of pairing apricots and Condrieu (Viognier), goat cheese and Sancerre (Sauvignon Blanc), oysters and Chablis (Chardonnay), lamb and red Bordeaux (Cabernet Sauvignon/Merlot), or mushrooms and red Burgundy (Pinot Noir). These are great launchpads. Try one of these pairings at home and see whether you feel the same way: fresh Dungeness crab and a chilled bottle of Chardonnay or grilled salmon and Pinot Noir. There you go, creating a new American culinary tradition!

> *White with light clothes. Red with dark clothes. Champagne without clothes, and beer with someone ugly.*
>
> —Sommelier's toast

Feeling frisky? Ask a French person to suggest a wine to go with a peanut butter and jelly sandwich studded with Doritos. Ha! That'll teach them.

Another philosophy centers on the concept of a bridge, which is built by adding the wine you are serving with the dish to the sauce, as in pairing a Chardonnay cream sauce with Chardonnay.

When choosing a wine to pair, consider the elements of the dish: protein, sauce, spice, and cooking technique. Imagine a plain, uncooked chicken breast is your protein. Now, imagine grilling it with a sweet tangy barbecue sauce, sautéing it with capers and butter, or oven-roasting it with garlic, sweet potatoes, white onions, and cream. Now, what wine goes with chicken?

Look at the upcoming grape chapters for specific food pairing suggestions. Keep in mind, too, that in the course of the meal, you will want to progress from lighter to fuller wines just as you would with the food.

SHOPPING: WINE AT RETAIL

When you are shopping in a grocery store, does someone come up to you and say, "This jar of pasta sauce is fruity, aromatic, and slightly sweet?" No. You look at the selection and either grab the one you are familiar with, grab the one that is on sale, or try something new. Think along these very same lines when shopping for wine.

Pick out two or three bottles that appeal to you and then ask a staff member for their opinion. If you like the tone and approach of this person, keep the dialogue going. It's your box full of Benjamins. If you feel pressured in any way, excuse yourself and walk out.

Try this with two or three wine shops, or wine sections in larger retail or upscale grocery stores that actually have floor staff to assist you. Visit often, without a plan. Just walk around and look at all the bottles. Pick up a newsletter if they have one, or check their website to see about in-store events, such as wine tastings. Going to in-store wine tastings, where allowed by law, is also the absolute best way to taste very exclusive and expensive high-end bottlings for a fraction of their cost. Ask the clerks which events they recommend. Eventually, if the chemistry is working for you, you will become a regular. Becoming a regular has tremendous rewards, as your clerk will become familiar with your lifestyle and tastes and will be able to turn you on to some great insider deals. Ask your merchant to recommend wines that have hidden value. Perhaps their names do not have a cult following. Perhaps the wine press didn't care for their unique style and balance as opposed to just all muscle and brawn. Experiment, explore, keep an open mind, and keep a journal so you remember what your discoveries are!

Eventually, when you know more about what you want, you can shop where service isn't as important and prices are lower. For example, maybe your clerk turned you on to a great $9 white. Stroll the aisles at Costco, Price Club, Cost Plus World Market, Total Wine & More, Beverages and More, or at any large chain outlet that carries wine, and keep your eyes peeled for that label and for other finds, including markdowns. If the chain buys that very same wine, it is buying in bulk, using its purchasing power to get a lower cost and then also taking slimmer markup. As it is selling in higher volume, you may pay $5 or $6 for the exact same bottle. Grocery Outlet is a chain specializing in closeouts. While there are plenty of regularly priced items, including wine, that are not bargains, they often buy out warehouses of wine inventory. Look for towers of wine boxes of the same brand, usually not in the wine section. These wines are often 60 to 80 percent off. Buy one, try it, and go back the same day to pick up more, otherwise it will be gone.

Let's take a closer look at pricing and how to get the best deal. Here's an example of a market survey I conducted recently:

Kendall-Jackson Vintner's Reserve Chardonnay California

$17.00	Winery Website and Tasting Room
$13.60	Wine Club Member Price
$13.99	Gourmet Grocery Store
$10.99	Wine.com
$10.97	Total Wine & More

As you can see, the lowest prices are at a huge online retailer (though shipping charges may apply) or at a chain.

Chain stores now also have their own private label wines, such as Target's California Roots, at $5 a bottle. Amazon has partnered with E. & J. Gallo to create its exclusive Proverb line, at $12.75 a bottle. The quality of these wines really depends on the decisions being made behind the scenes. I have not yet tasted them and so cannot recommend them. However, one of my jobs is sourcing for private label wines. If my name is on it, you can count on its quality.

In between the two extremes of full-service/high markup and no-service/low markup are a handful of wine shops that offer good service and discounted prices. K&L Wine Merchants (www.klwines.com) in California, and Binny's (www.binnys.com) in Chicago are two great examples.

Online shopping is an easy way to check prices and stumble on great deals.

You can search for just about anything, so type in "Chardonnay under $10" and see what comes up. You never know! Write down three examples of Chardonnay under $10 in your notebook. Leave room underneath each one for tasting notes. Now, if you can find the wines near you, check them out! By writing down your impressions, even a year later you'll be able to easily refresh your memory.

Specialty shops are another layer of wine merchants to consider. Certain wine buyers have an area they are crazy about, and they end up becoming specialists in the wines from that place. Whole Foods Market has a specialty collection of wines that are made with organically farmed fruit. Master Sommelier Devon Broglie and his team of regional buyers offer top-notch and well-priced selections from around the world. Perhaps a shop near you has a specialty selection that jibes with your tastes and preference.

You can also look on the back label of a wine you like, to see who the importer is. Write that name down, and ask for another wine from the same importer and see what you think. If you like them both, chances are you will enjoy many of this importer's selections.

Unless you really like the convenience of a few bottles showing up on your doorstep each month, wine-of-the-month clubs are typically not a good deal. First, you rely on someone else to pick out the wines, which are being mailed to everyone on the list regardless of personal preference. Even with claims of customizing to your tastes, the selections typically are industrial, not artisanal, and therefore not all that interesting. Second, you're paying a delivery fee, which raises the average price per bottle by up to one-third or more. Engage your local wine merchant or small, wine expert–guided online merchant instead for a more satisfying, customized, and value-for-your-dollar experience. Gary and Julia Marcaletti, owners of San Francisco Wine Trading Company, offer amazing customer care. They are constantly telling customers to buy less, not more, for weddings and such; if an older bottle is not in pristine condition, they won't let you buy it and will find something similar and offer it for the same price.

The world is your oyster. Take back that kid-in-a-candy-shop feeling. Shop with abandon, and always try something new. Employ what you've learned, and enjoy your experiences. Remember, wine is just fermented grape juice!

WHERE TO STORE IT

Once you extract the cork, wine begins to oxidize. Many whites will show the effects of this aging process within a few hours. Many of today's reds, however, especially those from the most recent vintage, may actually improve over a few days after opening just sitting on your kitchen counter. If the wine is a new-release red from California or Australia, if the retail price is above $15, and if it is a variety such as Cabernet Sauvignon, Merlot, or Cabernet Franc, not only will it last several days after opening, chances are it will improve. New-release California Pinot Noir and Syrah may lose some aromatics, but will also soften up over a day or two on the counter. A general rule of thumb is that the higher the acid and tannin (from oak and/or grape skins), the longer that wine will last open. Delicate and older wines tend to fade rather than improve. If the leftover wine is on the delicate side, put the cork back in and pop it in the fridge.

To keep wine fresh after opening and consuming part of the bottle, spray in Private Preserve, a nitrogen spray that blankets the wine and prevents contact with oxygen, available in fine wine shops. Avoid early pumping systems, such as Vacu Vin, as they extract delicate aromas and flavors along with the oxygen. More recently developed systems are gentler. I tested the Wine Doctor Classic and found it gentle and effective even on the most delicate wine.

The refrigerator isn't a good place to store unopened wine for more than a few months. Wine doesn't like being agitated by the constant vibration, which mutes character, and may lead to premature aging.

If you take a bottle of recent vintage Chardonnay from a reliable shop and place it in a lovely wine rack near direct light or heat, it may turn to vinegar in a matter of weeks. Take the same bottle and place it on its side in a dark, quiet, cool, and humid area, such as a basement or the very back of your closet, and it may stay fresh for a year or more.

Freestanding wine fridges or storage units are a fact of life for many folks, as are off-site wine storage facilities. Many wine merchants offer off-site storage starting at as little as $15 per month.

WINE IN RESTAURANTS

Typically people eat three times a day. Sometimes the meal is magic, and sometimes it is just sustenance. As often as we indulge our hunger and thirst, doesn't it seem odd that we aren't more comfortable with wine? After all, we are using the same eyes, nose, and mouth as we did at breakfast or lunch or dinner. We are using our sensorium. Wine has been ensconced too long in a cloud of mystery and superiority, reinforced as such classic television characters as Frasier and Niles vie for the title of "biggest wine bore of all time."

It can get even worse in fancy restaurants, where wine lists are as big as encyclopedias or as small as an iPad, and the jaded staff may be condescending. Take a deep breath, say to yourself, "It's my dime. I'm going to take my time," and dismiss Mr. Snooty Pants with the wave of a hand.

There is nothing I loathe more than a condescending sommelier. The best sommeliers are warm and friendly, and are knowledgeable but not intimidating. Like baristas in successful coffee shops, they know their beans, but they do not hold on to that knowledge for themselves. They are eager to educate you, not to look down their nose and sneer. Arrogance is so last century. The next time you encounter an arrogant sommelier, politely let them know you won't be requiring their services (tell them where to go) or contact me and I'll send in the Snob Squad!

The word *sommelier* (wine waiter) may stem from *bête de somme*—"beast of burden" in old French. The *sommelier* was its herdsman. By the fourteenth century, the word had become more specialized and referred to the official responsible for the transport of the French royalty's baggage when they traveled. By the eighteenth century in the household of a great lord, the sommelier was the official who chose the wines, table settings, and desserts. Early sommeliers were tasked with pretasting all food and drink for their master. If they died, their master knew not to consume the poisoned food or drink. Luckily, job conditions for sommeliers have greatly improved.

Set them straight: Somalia is a country in Africa, and is a word with four syllables. *Sommelier* is a word with three syllables. Try this: Say *summer*, then switch the *r* for an *l* and say *summel*. Now say, "Yay, the wine is here!"—"Summel-yay!"

grape goddess says:
"Summel-yay." Repeat after me: "Summel-yay."

While you might still cringe at the tongue-twisting, foreign word, at least today the odds are that you are much more likely to enjoy your experience with a sommelier. The modern wine steward is less intimidating, more approachable, and easier going than ever before. Tuxedos and tastevins, those big silver wine cups on a chain, are still around, but today's sommelier, even in the most formal dining room, is more likely to wear a suit and keep the silver tasting cup in a side pocket. Today's sommelier is also more likely than ever before to be female, and young.

The best sommeliers today are working to create a refreshingly open and wine-friendly atmosphere. They understand that fostering a fun, exciting wine culture works for both the novice and the experienced wine drinker. Most important, they remember that the primary focus of their job is to serve you.

It is all about you when you are a guest in a restaurant. Sit back, relax, and enjoy the ride! Formal restaurants know that you want to feel like a rock star when you come into their establishment, and will generally go out of their way to make this happen. With a little bit of homework, you can have the rock-star treatment even in casual establishments.

If you want to impress someone, scout out the scene beforehand. The easiest way to ensure a smooth flight is by going where you are known. Regulars get the upgrade to first class every time, especially if they tip well. If this is not possible, try to dine there at least once before the big day. At the very least, call and speak with the maître d' and the sommelier, if the establishment has one. Explain your plans. Tell them how important the occasion is. Tell them you will take care of them when you arrive—do so discreetly—and watch them treat you like royalty!

Corkage fees, charged when you bring in your own bottle, are an attempt to recoup some of the lost profit and are completely justified where sommelier service is offered. They range on average from $15 to $25, though a $50 corkage fee is not unheard of. Many restaurants in high-traffic areas don't allow corkage. Do not bring in multiple or large-format bottles. Check with the restaurant ahead of time about its corkage policy. Let the sommelier or manager know in advance—that is, when you make your reservation—that you are bringing a bottle in. It is good form to order one from the restaurant as well. You may also win points with your server and sommelier by offering them a taste of your wine. Bringing in wine is not nearly as bad as bringing in glassware. Unless the establishment is very casual and encourages this behavior, don't do it.

The best restaurant wine programs offer a selection of wines at all price points, especially in moderately priced selections, that work with the menu, that were chosen with a true passion, and that are offered up by warm, approachable servers, sommeliers, managers, and owners.

The wine list is just a list of the selections. If it intimidates you, close it and ask for the person who put it together. They may be the key to helping you make a good decision. Do you stress out this much when you are buying a steak? A tie? A new yoga mat? It is always completely acceptable to order a moderately priced wine. John Lancaster, sommelier at Boulevard Restaurant in San Francisco, says, "Sometimes I think the diner fears that the wine steward will simply try to sell him the most expensive wine. Exactly the opposite is the case. The sommelier is the builder of that list and will do everything to give you the best tour. Our goal is to put the right bottle of wine on the table, not the most expensive." If a commission-hungry sommelier is trying to sell you a wine out of your comfort zone, be firm and tell them to "come back in a few minutes."

Is it true that the more expensive a wine is, the better it will be? Absolutely not. Price is fairly irrelevant, especially at the ultra-premium level. You may prefer a $25 wine to a $125 wine. Only you can determine how much that pleasure is worth. A good rule of thumb is to spend twice as much on a bottle of wine as you do on the entrée.

You can expect to pay twice the retail price or more on most restaurant wine lists. If the wine is $20 at retail, it should be in the $40 range on a wine list. Each establishment will price according to its business model and philosophy. In general, the lowest-cost, entry-level wines are marked up the highest, whereas the pricier wines are marked up less. This is called a sliding scale.

Don't order the least expensive wines by the glass or bottle. This is where the highest markups are found. Go up $2 to $6 in a glass, or $8 to $12 in a bottle, and you will get a lot more bang for the buck. A sliding scale is used more often these days than a straight three-times markup, with the exception of resorts and country clubs. With the sliding-scale approach, the more the wine costs the restaurant, the lower the markup. More profit is made at the bottom end. The best deals are at the upper end. Reputable establishments that charge standard to high wine markups are covering the cost of wine storage and handling, glassware, decanters, and well-trained servers. Wine markups are a favorite target for restaurant critics, but they rarely talk about the price-to-cost ratio of a cocktail. For example, the vodka in a $17 martini may cost the establishment 70 cents.

For great value, look for older vintages, especially in well-established restaurants with a large wine cellar. Unless the restaurant has just acquired them at today's cost, these are hidden values. With more than four people order a magnum (1.5 L, or the equivalent of two 750 ml bottles). Magnums are impressive and may have a good price-to-value ratio. Plus, you just might get extra attention from your server or sommelier.

For business and for pleasure, think of your guests first. Don't worry about what they may think of you. Being honest and drawing them into the process is more impressive than pretending to know more than you do about wine. Also, depending on your rapport with the sommelier, ask him or her for suggestions, scanning your guests' faces as they make a recommendation. Ask your guests what they have liked in the past, what their favorites are. Get a feel for their tastes. Get them involved in the decision making. This is a win-win situation.

Ask what each of your guests is eating. If choices are all over the board, and if the selection is interesting and well priced, suggest, at least with the first course, that everyone choose a wine by the glass. Unless you have a good enough rapport with the group to bring everyone to a consensus, this is the least intrusive way to go. As the wine and conversation begin to flow, ordering additional wine may not present as many obstacles. Don't order a bottle of wine if you are not the host, unless the host has specifically asked you to do so.

If you'd like to take charge of the ordering, begin with an aperitif—an appetite-opener. Enlist your server's attention as soon as you sit down. In fact, when you arrive at the table, attempt right away to establish a rapport with your server and sommelier.

Ideal choices for aperitifs are sparkling wine or Champagne, or a dry, tart, appetite-stimulating wine, such as a French Sauvignon Blanc (Sancerre or Pouilly-Fumé from the Loire Valley) or a Sauvignon Blanc from California or New Zealand (ask for one that is not oaky). Order this immediately and ask that it be served right away. This helps to break the ice, slake the thirst, wash out the road dust, and set the tone for a convivial table.

What do you do if they hand you the cork? Smile and politely accept it. Look at it, roll it around in your hands, even squeeze it if you like. There is no need to sniff it, however, unless you enjoy the smell of natural cork bark or plastic. Just set it down, and hopefully the wine steward will ask to remove it from the table for you. This is one of the many traditions surrounding formal wine service. Since you are paying for the bottle, you have a right to watch the opening and cork extraction, and to physically examine it. Just keep in mind that the only way to tell whether your wine is corked (i.e., tainted by a natural compound, TCA, that presents as an off aroma of bleach or mold or mustiness), is to smell and taste the wine itself. I'll never forget watching Kevin Zraly demonstrating the cork scenario for his Windows on the World Wine School students. He told them that if they didn't know what to do with the cork, they could toss it at someone in the dining room who was annoying them! Naturally, he was kidding, but he made his point.

If you sense there is something wrong with the wine, engage the sommelier in a conversation about it, and make a quick decision. If there is something wrong with it, by all means, send back the wine as you would a piece of undercooked chicken. If you simply do not care for the wine, remember that your guests come first. Try to suck it up so that they are not kept waiting. The worst thing you can do is to send a wine back several minutes after you accepted it and had it poured into your glasses. Now there is no way for the restaurant to recoup the cost of that bottle. If you reject it at your first taste (and if the wine is not faulty—perhaps you just didn't care for it or it wasn't what you were expecting) the open bottle may be sold off by the glass, "comped" to regulars or VIPs, or tasted with the staff at the end of their shift. Be open, apologetic, charming, and frank.

A good sommelier will keep your glasses half full, and will be at the ready with additional bottles. The sommelier should present a new glass to the host with each new bottle, for the host to check for soundness. A top-notch sommelier will ask the host whether new glasses should be set around for each bottle, but this is not necessary if the wine is similar. When entertaining Europeans, however, be aware that there are certain superstitions about mixing different bottles of wine in the same glass. Also don't overlook dessert wines. Save room for a small sip of sweet nectar with or instead of dessert.

If you would like more (or less) wine in your glass, simply communicate this to your sommelier and server. Clearly state your preferences for having your wine topped up (or not) and how frequently, saying, "Don't let our glasses get empty" or "We'd like to enjoy our bottle slowly throughout our meal."

If you are pleased with the sommelier's service and would like to give them a little something extra, tip directly. It is rare that a sommelier is given a percentage of the server's gratuities, even if you indicate this on the check. If you order a very expensive bottle of wine and don't want to leave a standard tip on the bottle, simply say this to the sommelier and place cash in their hand. If you are not pleased with your sommelier, let them know, and let their bosses know, too, either verbally or, to be really effective, by sending a note.

What do you do when faced with a snooty sommelier? Take a deep breath, try to relax, and concentrate on the fact that you are the one spending the money. You are the customer. Remember, it's your dime. Take your time. When you are faced with sommeliers who pride themselves on their knowledge of irrelevant minutiae about wine, try your very special extra best to establish a rapport. Think of something to make them crack a smile. I know you can do it.

TEN
GRAPES
TO KNOW

PINOT GRIS/GRIGIO

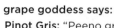

grape goddess says:
Pinot Gris: "Peeno gree." Repeat after me: "Peeno gree."
Pinot Grigio: "Peeno gree-joe." Repeat after me: "Peeno gree-joe."

Pinot Grigio provides the soothing comfort of an old friend. There are no surprises. It is what it is and it hasn't changed in years. It is shy, dry, fresh, and delightfully unfruity, the absolute antithesis of a big, buttery Chardonnay. Like an old friend, it may be a bit nutty on occasion. Or a bit salty or even bitter. Come on, admit it. You have a friend just like this.

Known as Pinot Grigio in Italy and Pinot Gris in France, this grape has wide appeal for its very lack of fruit. People love it because it doesn't demand attention. It is easygoing and chill. Producers in the New World choose one name or the other based on the style they are emulating.

My fellow Master Sommeliers like to take potshots at Pinot Grigio. They constantly tease me about defending it. I am a huge fan. After a long day of presenting, my mouth is parched and I don't want to have to think about or process what I am drinking. While I love the bright, zesty punch of a Sauvignon Blanc; ripe, tropical tones of a Viognier; and the creamy texture of Chardonnay, sometimes I am just not in the mood. Pinot Grigio is low maintenance.

Due in large part to where it is grown, Pinot Gris is a weightier, riper expression of this grape, often presented with a touch of sweetness that nicely counteracts the grape's inherent bitterness. Pinot Gris production is a fraction of that of Pinot Grigio.

HISTORY

Pinot Gris/Grigio is an evolution (mutation) of Pinot Noir. Originating from Burgundy, France, where it is known as Pinot Beurot, Pinot Gris has a pinkish-grayish skin (*gris* for "gray"). While Chardonnay is the white grape of Burgundy, until very recently there were a handful of remaining plantings of Pinot Gris there, the most famous being a tiny plot on the hill of Corton. It was used in Champagne in the past, and still is to a small degree in California sparkling wine.

When the wine is produced with skin contact, it will have a light copper to fully rosé color. In the 1980s and '90s, this was the style favored by Oregonian winemakers, but sadly it lost favor with consumers, who preferred the rich golden yellow Chardonnays popular at the time. The golden yellow color is a result of extended barrel aging. Today the copper-tinged style is making a global comeback, riding no doubt on the wild popularity of rosé (see page 108).

Ten Grapes to Know

GEOGRAPHY

It is hard to believe that rich, honeyed, tangy, minerally Alsatian Pinot Gris from France is related to neutral, quaffable Italian Pinot Grigio. This grape ripens early and drops acidity fast, with lower acidity resulting in a creaminess and richness similar to, say, a white Burgundy (Chardonnay). Since they are not aged in oak, these wines go to market as soon as three months after harvest.

The best Old World Pinot Gris is produced in Alsace, France, where long sunny summer days provide ideal ripening conditions and the wines are rich, opulent, and

PINOT GRIS/GRIGIO AT A GLANCE

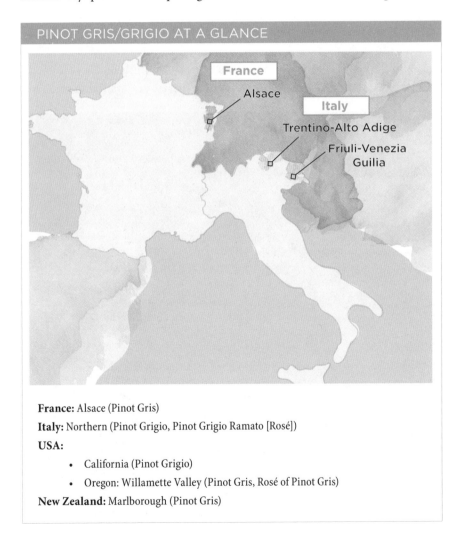

France: Alsace (Pinot Gris)

Italy: Northern (Pinot Grigio, Pinot Grigio Ramato [Rosé])

USA:

- California (Pinot Grigio)
- Oregon: Willamette Valley (Pinot Gris, Rosé of Pinot Gris)

New Zealand: Marlborough (Pinot Gris)

sometimes lightly sweet. The best Old World Pinot Grigios come from the northeast Italian alpine areas of Collio and Colli Orientali near Udine in Friuli-Venezia Giulia, and from the Trentino-Alto Adige, where they showcase a smoky minerality—as in actually smelling of rocks. Go to your nearest garden center and take a sniff. To provide the racy, lemony-fresh style of wines the country loves, Italian winemakers pick early while the grape still has high levels of natural acidity. At this time, the grape sugars are not as high, so the resulting alcohol levels will be lower as well.

Thanks in part to the popularity of Italian restaurant chains in the United States, California producers enjoy a large demand for Italian varietals and thus for the most part label their wines as Pinot Grigio. Oregon's Willamette Valley was an early Pinot Gris growing area. They wanted to be known for something other than Chardonnay and did quite well with Pinot Noir, so they looked to Pinot Gris produced in the Alsatian style. Pinot Gris ripens beautifully on New Zealand's warmer North Island and cooler South Island, especially in Marlborough.

THE GIANT CHAIR

On a press trip in Friuli a few years back, I got to meet some great wine-producing families, tasting bright, fresh, tart wines and eating a lot of prosciutto di San Daniele and polenta. I loved to get up early and walk along the cobblestone streets and arched bridges in Gorizia before getting on the shuttle bus. On the way out of town, we always passed a giant wooden chair in the middle of a traffic circle. It had to be over two stories high. We learned that this was the marker for the Italian Chair District, where the chair as we know it today was invented in the fifteenth century. This area is still the chair-making capital of Europe.

By this time in my career I had heard about and sat on the Rutherford Bench, an oversize bench in front of Franciscan Winery in Rutherford, Napa Valley. This was their tongue-in-cheek way of celebrating the Rutherford bench-growing area. A bench in geographical terms is where the base of the hill meets the valley floor. But this giant Italian chair was something else!

We grew to enjoy the long bus rides home from the day's visits. We talked about Casanova, castles, and the chair. Casanova often had encounters at Castello di Spessa in Collio. After lunch there one visit, I asked the chef what Casanova ate. He replied, "I am old, but not that old!" Just as we grew weary of the ride someone would call out, "There's the chair!" We were relieved, as this meant we were close to the hotel. We'd ride a few more moments, and then, "There's the chair!" Our drivers either were new or didn't know exactly where we were going. There was no GPS at that time.

TASTE PROFILE AND STYLES

Pinot Gris from Alsace, France, offers the silkiness and sumptuousness of Burgundy along with honeyed notes, tanginess, and a chalky minerality. Rare and pricey late-harvest versions are worth seeking out.

At its most basic quality, Italian Pinot Grigio is neutral, dry, tart, crisp, or even bracing, like a wave crashing down on a hot summer day. It beautifully quenches the thirst while leaving one ready to eat. At its most complex it is still neutral, if a bit more interesting. I love the lemony freshness, salinity, and bitter finish of a good Italian Pinot Grigio. Rosé of Pinot Grigio has a light raspberry note and is bone dry as well.

In the USA, commercial producers tend to either lavishly oak their wines in an effort to appeal to the Chardonnay crowd or to leave the wines slightly sweet, or both. Pinot Grigio is planted everywhere, and may even be labeled as American Pinot Grigio. Likely this will be simple and sweet. Better California and Oregon Pinot Gris wines often have a very light touch of sweetness.

In general, the New Zealand style emulates the honeyed, lightly sweet Alsatian style. "New Zealand dry," according the locals, is lightly sweet. Another reason to love the place!

SENSE EXERCISE

Get to Know Your Palate

Spread a teaspoon of almond butter on small piece of sourdough toast. Is this to your liking?

Take a sip of lemon water, then add a drop of honey and take another sip. Which version do you prefer?

These are excellent ways to get to know your palate and help you hone in on wine styles you will really enjoy. When you are interacting with a wine merchant in person or chatting online, as in at Wine.com, explain to the person that you love the tartness of lemon or the sweetness of honey. Or admit that you pour half-and-half on your Cheerios. Or that you like your coffee black, or with sugar, and so on. Once they understand some of your palate preferences, they can lead you to styles of wine you may enjoy.

MATCHMAKING

Wines that are fruit-neutral are easy to pair with food. Of all the wines they produce, the Alsatians prefer to serve Pinot Gris with their dishes; Italian Pinot Grigio goes even further. With its brisk acidity and touch of bitterness, it can take on rich white sauces, bitter greens, and citrusy and even garlicky dishes.

EVERY DAY WITH PINOT GRIS

Pork schnitzel (dry Pinot Gris)
Grilled cheese sandwich with eggplant and Swiss (dry Pinot Gris)
Foie gras (dry Vendange Tardive Pinot Gris)
Peach tart (sweet Vendange Tardive or SGN Pinot Gris)

EVERY DAY WITH PINOT GRIGIO

Crab cakes

Tuna chickpea arugula salad

Prosciutto and melon

Shrimp scampi

Scallop risotto

Quinoa with butternut squash

Root vegetable gratin

Grilled eggplant and hummus wrap

INSTA DINNER

Lean Cuisine—Roasted Garlic White Bean
   Alfredo

Lean Cuisine—Lemon Chicken

Trader Joe's—frozen pork gyoza

Takeout—sesame chicken

UPSCALE CONVENIENCE

Homemade by Ayesha Curry—Vegetable Ratatouille over Creamy Polenta

SNACK

Garlic fries or sweet potato fries

> ### Skin Contact for Rosé
> Winemaker Andrew Kirkland of Ruby Vineyard in Willamette Valley, Oregon, observed firsthand while working in Australia that skin contact, leaving the freshly fermented grape must (wine) in contact with the grape skins for nine days, not only brings the *gris*, or copper, color to the wine, but also adds flesh and body, like an actor gaining weight for a role. Enjoy this vineyard's Willamette Valley Rosé of Pinot Gris the next time you are yachting—or watching Netflix.

DINNER TONIGHT

CHICKEN CORDON BLEU

Grab this frozen dinner at the supermarket and pop it in the oven while you chill a bottle of light, silky, and fresh Hugel Pinot Gris, Alsace $24.

FETTUCCINE WITH PANCETTA

Boil the pasta, fry up some pancetta or bacon, add a dash of cream, and enjoy with a glass of steely, crisp, tart, and dry Terlato Pinot Grigio, Colli Orientali, Friuli $25.

SHOPPING

Pinot Gris and Pinot Grigio wines are easy on the wallet. Even inexpensive Pinot Grigios are suitable for entertaining, as their style is neutral and crisp, very quaffable. That being said, it is always a good idea to look closely at the origin. Better wines are typically labeled with more specific regions. Whereas a wine labeled "Pinot Grigio, Carneros" or "Pinot Grigio, California" should be fresh and dry, one labeled "Pinot Grigio, America" likely will be sweet. This style should be

labeled as "Pinot Gris" to give folks an idea of style, but since Pinot Grigio is a brisk seller, many producers go with that version of the grape name. Keep in mind that when a producer is blending fruit from sources that may be less than ideal, it is using additives, such as sugar, to improve the taste and texture.

Ditto for Pinot Grigio from Italy. Where is it from? Good geographical names to look for are Trentino, Alto Adige, Friuli, Venezia Giulia, and Dolomiti.

As with other types of wine, when shopping for Pinot Grigio, stay clear of labels that are too bright or gimmicky. I like Pinot Grigio that is bone dry, crisp, and tart. Why would I buy one with a cupcake on the label?

Wines labeled as Pinot Gris are not so problematic, as their production levels are much lower. In Alsace, quality is very high across the board and production is low, with most producers artisanal, not industrial in scale. As a result, for around $20 you will get a delightful, balanced, expressive wine.

EVERYDAY VALUE/SHOPPING UNDER $20

Italy

Bella Sera Pinot Grigio, Veneto $8

Fruity and fresh with notes of white peach, nectarine, guava, ginger, and lime zest

Bertani Velante Pinot Grigio, Venezia Giulia $14

Crisp, delicate, and dry with notes of melon, ginger, lemon pound cake, and almond butter

Bottega Vinaia Pinot Grigio, Trentino $18

Soft, juicy, light, and dry with notes of lemon wafer, starfruit, cashew, and chalk

Cavit Pinot Grigio, delle Venezie $9

Light and crisp with notes of lemon, peach skin, muskmelon, and violet

Ecco Domani Pinot Grigio, delle Venezie $12

Dry, tart, and fresh with notes of lemon, lime, apricot, chalk, and honeysuckle

Hofstätter Pinot Grigio, Alto Adige $19

Light, dry, and tart with notes of lemon preserve, pine needle, and sea salt

Riff Pinot Grigio, delle Venezie $10

Light, crisp, and very dry with notes of lemon zest, lanolin, and sea salt

Sartori di Verona Pinot Grigio, delle Venezie $13

Light, tart, dry, and zesty with notes of lemon, peach, almond, and sea salt

Tiefenbrunner Pinot Grigio, Vigneti delle Dolomiti $18

Midweight, dry, creamy, and austere with notes of lemon, gin and tonic, and chalk

USA

The Naked Grape Pinot Grigio, California $18/3 L box

Dry, tart, and subtle with notes of lemon, Golden Delicious apple, tangerine, and bay leaf

Montinore Estate Pinot Gris, Willamette Valley $16

Ripe, vibrant, and lightly chewy with notes of peach, pear, pink rose, ginger, and pine nut (Demeter Certified Organic)

Pike Road Pinot Gris, Willamette Valley $15

Soft and fresh with notes of lemon curd, Red Delicious apple, honeycomb, and orange blossom

Willamette Valley Vineyards Pinot Gris, Willamette Valley $17

Creamy, light, and dry with notes of lemon curd, apricot jam, almond slivers, and vanilla

New Zealand

Villa Maria Private Bin Pinot Gris, East Coast $15

Tingly, lightly sweet, and fresh with notes of lemon zest, peach yogurt, ginger, rose water, and whole wheat pretzel

IMPRESS YOUR GUESTS/SHOPPING $20-$50

France

Domaine Schlumberger Les Princes Abbés Pinot Gris, Alsace $20

Round, tangy, and slightly sweet with notes of lemon curd, almond slivers, bear claw pastry, sourdough bread, ginger ale, and quinine

Hugel Pinot Gris, Alsace $24

Light, silky, and fresh with notes of lemon meringue, apple tart, rising bread, ginger, and almond

Pierre Sparr Pinot Gris Grande Réserve, Alsace $20

Creamy then pithy, tart then sweet, with notes of honey, lime juice, peach pit, and almond slivers

Italy

Alois Lageder Pinot Grigio Porer, Alto Adige $25

Full, tingly, dry, and tart with notes of lemon, pink grapefruit, tangerine, and sea spray

Attems Pinot Grigio Ramato (Rosé), Venezia Giulia $20

Silky, light, and tart rosé with notes of lemon, raspberry, strawberry, and violet

Maso Canali Pinot Grigio, Trentino $23

Clean and delicate with notes of lemon zest, pear, white pepper, ginger, and chalk

Terlato Family Pinot Grigio, Friuli $25

Steely, crisp, tart, and dry with notes of lemon zest, tangerine, celery, chamomile, and chalk

Villa Russiz Pinot Grigio, Collio $26

Feather light, crisp, and bone dry with notes of lemon meringue, just-ripe pear, chamomile, and talc

USA

Chanticleer Pinot Grigio, Carneros, Napa Valley $30

Soft, silky, and dry with notes of lemon crème, apricot, sourdough crust, biscotti with almonds, and lanolin

J Vineyards Pinot Gris, Russian River Valley, Sonoma $23

Medium-bodied, juicy, and refreshing with notes of pear, lemongrass, and honeydew melon

Merisi Pinot Gris, Los Carneros, Sonoma $24

Soft, rich, silky, and fresh with notes of lemon meringue pie, mandarin, honeysuckle, and ginger

Ruby Vineyard Rosé of Pinot Gris, Willamette Valley $20

Dry and refreshing with notes of strawberry, rhubarb, and green tea

New Zealand

Loveblock Pinot Gris, Marlborough $22

Juicy and sweet-tart with notes of lemon, almond cookie, ginger, and honeysuckle

Spy Valley Pinot Gris, Marlborough $24

Softly sweet and plump with notes of lemon drop, ginger wafer, almond sliver, and honeysuckle

WORTH THE SPLURGE/SHOPPING $50 AND ABOVE

France

Hugel Pinot Gris Grossi Laüe, Alsace $95

Full, creamy, bold, and bright with notes of tangerine, lanolin, dried herbs, and crème fraîche

SANTA MARGHERITA

Tony Terlato is called the "father of Pinot Grigio" for introducing Americans to this grape in 1979. Tony's overnight success with Santa Margherita Pinot Grigio took 20 years of working the market relentlessly. All of sudden people—and by people, I mean women—were ordering the sophisticated sounding but easy-to-pronounce light, dry, crisp white wine. Did they care it was Italian? Did they even know what grape it was? Likely not. Santa Margherita was the "it" wine of the '90s and early 2000s and is still popular all over the world. It was, however, a tad pricey for my tastes, often coming in at double comparable Pinot Grigios that were far less glamorous. You can say the same thing about Veuve Clicquot Champagne. Nice Champagne, better marketing—its ubiquitous orange label is iconic. About two years ago, Terlato sold the Santa Margherita brand and has since partnered with Italian viticulturalists Marco Simonit and Pierpaolo Sirch to produce Terlato Pinot Grigio Friuli with grapes grown in the ideal Colli Orientali (hills in the Alps that face the East [the Orient]). Tony's sons Bill, Tony, and John are all involved in the family business today.

OLIVIER HUMBRECHT, MW

Domaine Zind-Humbrecht, Alsace, was created in 1959 by two winegrowing families, the Humbrecht family from Gueberschwihr and the Zind family from Wintzenheim. Before 1959, both families produced and commercialized their wines under their respective family names. Today the Domaine is run by Olivier and Margaret Humbrecht. In 1997 the Domaine started producing biodynamic grapes by following the strict rules of biodynamic farming, which are more comprehensive than those for farming organically, or naturally. Biodynamic farming takes into account the environment, people, animals, and resources.

DINING OUT

Unlike most other European wines, both Pinot Grigio from Italy and Pinot Gris from Alsace have the grape right in the name, so that will make it easier to find them as a group. In Italy, Pinot Grigio had huge commercial success based on the easy-to-say and easy-to-remember grape name and so they crafted the law to accommodate labeling with its grape name. In the case of Pinot Gris, as Alsace went back and forth as German and then French territory, when it finally was integrated into France, the French recognized the high quality of the wines but required they "disclose" the name of the German grape, Riesling, so folks would know they were getting a German grape. The law was written to ensure all wines in Alsace were labeled with their grape type.

> ### How Sweet It Is
> Wines labeled as Pinot Grigio from Italy will be dry to bone dry. Wines labeled as Pinot Grigio from California and Oregon will be dry to slightly sweet. Wines labeled as Pinot Gris from New Zealand tend to fall more in line with the Alsatian styles, which range from dry to decadently sweet. Some producers in Alsace and other parts of the world have added a sweetness indicator to their back labels.

Engage the sommelier, or refer to my recommended wines, but don't be afraid to experiment, and don't be afraid to send a wine back if you think it is not good.

BRANCH OUT

WHITE BURGUNDY

From Pinot Gris, go to white Burgundy (French Chardonnay), such as Meursault or Mâcon. Try the Réserve des Rochers, Mâcon-Chaintré $17, a crisp, silky and subtle Chardonnay with notes of lemon peel, lemon leaf, chalk, and coriander. Read more about white Burgundy on page 64.

SOAVE

From Pinot Grigio, go to Soave from Veneto, Italy. I recommend the Bertani Sereole Soave $16, light, mellow, and dry with notes of lemon, lanolin, and banana pudding.

THE ALLIGATOR

"Riff" is short and simple, easy to pronounce and easy to remember. Easier in fact than the family name. That is why from the moment I heard the term *alligator* for "Al Lageder" 28 years ago, I knew I'd never forget it. To this day I use it as a staff training tool and you can bet it helps boost sales. At a recent luncheon in San Francisco's Chinatown with Alois Clemens Lageder and Jo Pfisterer, I shared the story. Al was intrigued. He had never heard this before!

From my earliest days as a sommelier at Windows on the World, I glommed on to any little play on words that would ease pronunciation, for my work, and memorization, for my studies and exams. It was there in 1989 that I first learned about Alois Lageder, a family-owned winery in Alto Adige near Trento in northeastern Italy. Johann Lageder founded the winery in 1832. Today the winery is run by Alois and his son Alois Clemens, representing the fifth and sixth generation. They farm biodynamically, and with the help of winemaker Jo Pfisterer, produce a wide range of white and red wines, with a special focus on Pinot Grigio. Jo likes the tension acid brings to the wine, and when the vintage is warmer, he will use grape skin contact to bring it back.

Ten years ago, Alois and his son launched Cantina Riff Pinot Grigio, an entry-level wine with fruit from growers across the Veneto south of Trento and closer to the city of Venice. The vineyard sources for the wine are located throughout the most northern part of the Veneto region, which stretches from the majestic Dolomite peaks in the north, to the Veneto's rolling farmland in the foothills of the Alps and around Lake Garda, to Friuli's hills in the east. This triumvirate's geography, topography, and unique climate conditions are undoubtedly Mediterranean but benefit from a cooling alpine influence in the evening, creating ideal growing conditions for Pinot Grigio.

Alois Lageder partners with quality, experienced winegrowers to produce this wine and in exchange, he shares their knowledge, experience, and expertise in viticulture and winemaking, among which is growing grapes organically. The goal is to help each vineyard become organic in the future.

2

SAUVIGNON BLANC

grape goddess says:
"So-vin-yon blahnk." Repeat after me: "So-vin-yon blahnk."

Sauvignon Blanc is one of the world's most beloved grapes and is planted all over the globe. This was not always the case. First known to Americans in the 1960s as sophisticated if lean and tart French sippers, Sancerre and Pouilly-Fumé (say "pwee foo-may") still enjoy a following today and are classic offerings at every French bistro or restaurant.

Just as Malbec has reached its fullest potential not in the south of France but rather on the snow-covered terraces of Argentina, so, too, has cool but sunny New Zealand birthed a wine so wildly popular it has changed the landscape. Marlborough, New Zealand, has absolutely nailed Sauvignon Blanc.

HISTORY

While British wine writer and former West End actor Oz Clarke likes to say the history of Sauvignon Blanc began with the first plantings in New Zealand in 1973, folks in South West France, Bordeaux, and the Loire Valley would beg to differ, claiming it as native to their area. The name "Sauvignon" derives from *sauvage*, or "wild." It is the "mother" of Cabernet Sauvignon, and in fact, old records list these two as Sauvignon Blanc and Sauvignon.

GEOGRAPHY

France is the historic birthplace of Sauvignon Blanc. From the Loire Valley south of Paris, we see smoky, flinty Pouilly-Fumé and from across the banks of the Loire River, subtle, lemony tart Sancerre. Both are grown in rocky soils in a very cool climate. This is Sauvignon Blanc at its least ripe and most minerally. Sauvignon Blanc plays a minor role in both dry white Bordeaux and Sauternes, the sweet wine of the area. Both of those are commonly based on the richer, rounder, and more neutrally flavored Sémillon grape, which benefits greatly from combination with Sauvignon Blanc's lithe zestiness.

Northern Italian vineyards near Trieste in Friuli-Venezia Giulia and in Trentino-Alto Adige are sources of lean, racy styles of Sauvignon Blanc. Northern and central California produce a variety of styles, and from northern and central coastal valleys in Chile, we see the closest thing to Sancerre but at half the price.

Producers all over the world are following the tremendous success of the lively, expressive New Zealand versions. The engine room of New Zealand wine is Marlborough, on the South Island, a cool but extremely sunny area with a variety of soil types giving a rainbow of ripeness that, when blended together, produces a seamless, thrilling, refreshing wine.

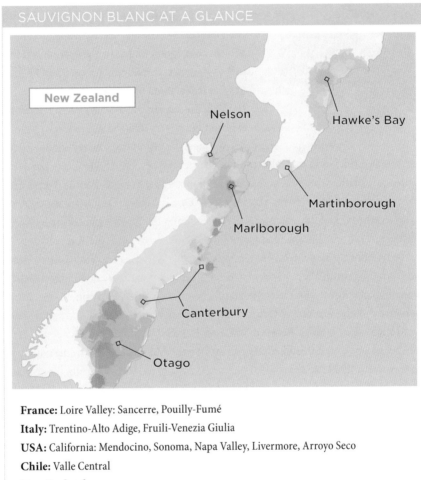

France: Loire Valley: Sancerre, Pouilly-Fumé
Italy: Trentino-Alto Adige, Fruili-Venezia Giulia
USA: California: Mendocino, Sonoma, Napa Valley, Livermore, Arroyo Seco
Chile: Valle Central
New Zealand:
- South Island: Marlborough, Nelson, Canterbury, Central Otago
- North Island: Hawke's Bay, Martinborough

TASTE PROFILE AND STYLES

From the Old World, or cold world, neighbors Sancerre and Pouilly-Fumé in France's Loire Valley produce light, tart, and sometimes floral wines that are racy, lean, and chalky. Pouilly-Fumés are generally a bit pricier and occasionally mellow out in oak before being bottled. They sometimes too have a stronger, smokier, gunflint type of minerality. From Friuli-Venezia Giulia and Alto Adige in northern Italy, the Sauvignon Blancs are less green and less fruity, closer in style to a really good Pinot Grigio, but with just a touch of green zestiness.

In the beginning of the modern California wine era, Sauvignon Blanc was made as a nondescript semi-sweet wine. Then came pioneering visionary Robert Mondavi, who had traveled the world to understand its greatest wines. He decided to make a dry Sauvignon Blanc, which he called Fumé Blanc, a reference to Pouilly-Fumé. The word *fumé* has two translations from French. One is "smoky," implying strong gunflint minerality, and the other is "toasty," implying the flavors and textures of new toasted oak barrels. Because the name Fumé Blanc is unregulated and used at will, it doesn't offer up any clues as to the wine's style. Wineries use the name to stand out from the crowd. Their wines may be crisp and dry, mellow and lightly sweet, or even obviously oaky with flavors of vanilla bean or coconut. Early on, Robert Mondavi Fumé Blanc was one of California's finest Sauvignon Blancs. Today, the Robert Mondavi Fumé Blanc Reserve To Kalon I Block Napa Valley, a decadently rich, creamy, toasty, and full-bodied wine from 54-year-old vines, is one of the country's best. Another iconic wine is the Dry Creek Vineyard DCV3 Sauvignon Blanc made with 24-year-old vines at its estate in Dry Creek Valley, Sonoma.

I am a huge fan of Chilean Sauvignon Blancs from Casablanca Valley as well as nearby San Antonio's Leyda Valley and Aconcagua. These cool coastal valleys produce dry, crisp, and lightly fruity styles more in line with the French than the New Zealand styles and are extremely well priced. Even wines labeled as Valle Central (Central Valley), Chile, with nothing more specific can provide easy enjoyment.

I love Oz Clarke's description of New Zealand's brash, pungent Sauvignon Blanc, an iconic style created by Cloudy Bay winemaker Kevin Judd. He calls it a "cloudburst, thrilling, shocking, lime zest, capsicum, love me or leave me" style of Sauvignon Blanc. Judd, who produced the Cloudy Bay's first 25 vintages and who now has his own winery, Greywacke, had no idea this blend of underripe green and superripe

As a singer, Sauvignon Blanc would be Adam Levine of Maroon 5. A crisp white shirt lends an air of polish to even the edgiest rock star, covering the full-sleeve tats and chains.

- I am lively, exuberant, and the life of the party.
- I am fun, high energy, and love to dance.
- I like to be the center of attention.
- If I grow up without much sun, I am lean, edgy, tart, and shy.
- If I grow up with a lot of sun, I am passionate and spicy!
- I am refreshing and lighthearted. I will make you smile.

tropical flavors would take the world by storm. His innovation was to blend in the green, tart, early-picked wine his crew loved so much with fruit picked just ripe as well as some that was overripe and tropical. It is common to find varying levels of ripeness within the vineyards at the same time, due to the variety of soil types there.

Now some winemakers are dialing back on these opulent flavors, both the tropical passion fruit and pineapple and Sauvignon Blanc's signature zesty green and herbaceous notes. These days, quality-conscious producers are focusing on textural elements they can manipulate by using such winemaking techniques as stirring the lees/yeast sediment, and aging in barrel. Most of the New Zealand Sauvignon Blanc on the market never sees oak. Zesty green vegetal flavors and oak are very antagonistic—oak can elevate the pungent greenness to a point where they clash.

If the output of the vine is lower than normal—say, your tomato plant gave you 20 small tomatoes rather than 40—each resulting fruit is more flavorful and complex. Take this complex fruit, age for a short time in neutral older oak—no need for oak vanillins or chewy barrel tannins—and the wine stretches out and breathes a little, becoming more mellow and creamy, less edgy. Giesen's "The Fuder" series, named in honor of the German beer barrel and from selected single vineyard sites, is an impressive lineup of this style of Sauvignon Blanc.

Marlborough produces the quintessential style the world has come to love. Marlborough's Wairau Valley is the most prolific, but the wines from the Awatere Valley to the southeast have a bracing liveliness, like a refreshing splash from a breaking wave. In nearby Nelson, a bohemian artist community, Sauvignon Blanc is slightly mellower. Toward Christchurch, Canterbury produces bright juicy wines. In Central Otago to the south near Queenstown, the wines are peachy and fresh. On the North Island, Hawke's Bay on the east coast produces supple, rounded wines, while Martinborough near Wellington produces a fresh, lively, and spicy style.

MATCHMAKING

Sauvignon Blanc is refreshing on its own and easy to pair with a wide variety of foods. Most of it is light, tart, and unoaked. There is a natural affinity with herbs or softly flavored green vegetables. A little spice or heat is okay, too.

EVERY DAY WITH SAUVIGNON BLANC

Steamed mussels with Sauvignon Blanc, lemon, and coriander

Fresh oysters with a squeeze of lemon

Fish tacos

Fritto misto

Lemon chicken with asparagus

CHEESE

Goat cheese—chèvre/Crottin de Chavignol or locally produced

Swiss/Emmentaler

INSTA DINNER

Lean Cuisine—Butternut Squash Ravioli

Trader Joe's—Pesto and Quinoa with your favorite pasta or chicken

Takeout—fish & chips

UPSCALE CONVENIENCE

Blue Apron—Summer Vegetable Quesadillas with Roasted Sweet Potatoes and Lime Sour Cream

SNACK

Chile-lime peanuts, popcorn, or wings

Smoked salmon

Grab a bag of prewashed mixed greens, precooked and cut chicken, crumbled goat cheese, slivered almonds, and Italian salad dressing. Assemble and serve with the fresh, light, and billowy Villa Maria Private Bin Sauvignon Blanc, Marlborough $15, or the delicate, silky, crisp and dry Vincent Vatan Pouilly-Fumé Selection Silex $22.

SHOPPING

EVERYDAY VALUE/SHOPPING UNDER $20

Italy

Cembra Cantina di Montagna, Trentino $14

Light, dry, and very crisp with soft notes of peach, white rose, spring pea, basil, and thyme

Manincor Tannenberg Sauvignon, Terlano, Alto Adige $16

Soft, subtle, and tart with notes of dried herbs, sea spray, white peach, and apricot

Prodigo Sauvignon Blanc, Friuli Grave $11

Silky, soft, and fresh with notes of white peach, cantaloupe, green pea, asparagus, chervil, and chalk

USA

Cannonball Sauvignon Blanc, Sonoma $16

Silky, smooth, and subtle with notes of pink grapefruit, thyme, spring pea, pink peppercorn, and lemon zest

Ferrari-Carano Fumé Blanc, Sonoma $14

Soft, pithy, and dry with notes of dried herbs, peach, and ginger

Gallo Family Vineyards Sauvignon Blanc, California $4

Clean, fresh, and lightly sweet with notes of apricot, lemongrass, oregano, and chive

J Lohr Sauvignon Blanc Flume Crossing, Arroyo Seco $14

Lively and zesty with notes of guava, pear, pink peppercorn, and tarragon

Paul Dolan Vineyards Sauvignon Blanc, Potter Valley $15

Full, soft, fresh, and nearly dry with notes of lemon crème, peach, vanilla custard, and white chocolate (made with organically grown grapes)

Wente Vineyards Sauvignon Blanc Louis Mel, Livermore Valley $15

Bright, lemony, and zesty with notes of peach, passion fruit, mango, pine needle, and lemongrass

Chile

Cousiño Macul Sauvignon Blanc, Central Valley $11

Brisk and dry with notes of Bosc pear, peach skin, lemongrass, basil, and thyme

De Martino Estate Sauvignon Blanc, Casablanca Valley $16

Round, supple, and fresh with notes of lime zest, peach, guava and sage

Miguel Torres Sauvignon Blanc Las Mulas, Central Valley $10

Juicy and refreshing with notes of green apple, peach, star fruit, and dried herbs

Santa Rita Secret Reserve Sauvignon Blanc, Casablanca Valley $11

Fresh, lively, crisp, and dry with notes of cantaloupe, mango, papaya, black pepper, and bell pepper

Veramonte Sauvignon Blanc, Casablanca Valley $12

Crisp, dry, and refreshing with notes of cantaloupe, guava, bay leaf, sage, and white pepper

New Zealand

Glazebrook Regional Reserve Sauvignon Blanc, Marlborough $15

Vivid, light, and clean with notes of kumquat, navel orange, nettle, and leek

Hunter's Sauvignon Blanc, Marlborough $16

Light, delicate, fresh, and dry with notes of lime zest, lemongrass, peach, papaya, and pink peppercorn

Kim Crawford Sauvignon Blanc, Marlborough $18

Crisp, vivid, tingly, and nearly austere with notes of lemongrass, oregano, spring pea, chive, lime, honeydew, cantaloupe, and ripe pineapple

Matua Sauvignon Blanc, Marlborough $15

Clean, fresh, and dry with notes of lime, tangelo, peach, lemongrass, and chive

Mohua Sauvignon Blanc, Marlborough $16

Crisp, fresh, light, and dry with notes of peach, pineapple, lemongrass, spring pea, and white pepper

Nautilus Estate Sauvignon Blanc, Marlborough $15

Light and chalky with notes of peach, pineapple, celery, cucumber, wax bean, and mushroom

Peter Yealands Sauvignon Blanc, Marlborough $15

A lively, refreshing trifecta of fruit, herbal, and mineral notes

Sea Pearl Sauvignon Blanc, Marlborough $12

Crisp, fresh, racy, and dry with notes of pink grapefruit, spring pea, rosemary, and dill

Starborough Sauvignon Blanc, Marlborough $17

Crisp, light, and nearly dry with notes of lime zest, peach, guava, and yellow rose

Villa Maria Sauvignon Blanc Private Bin, Marlborough $15

Fresh, light, and billowy with notes of lemongrass, white pepper, thyme, rosemary, peach, guava, and dried pineapple

Seifried Sauvignon Blanc, Nelson $18

Racy and pungent with notes of green and red bell pepper, canned peas, mustard greens, and watermelon rind

Mt. Beautiful Sauvignon Blanc, North Canterbury $16

Vividly fruity, lightly herby, spicy, and fresh with notes of lime zest, peach, mango, pineapple rind, spring pea, and Thai red chile skin

Carrick Sauvignon Blanc, Central Otago $18

Clean and bracing with notes of lime zest, white pepper, peach, and passion fruit

IMPRESS YOUR GUESTS/SHOPPING $20-$50

France

Domaine Vacheron Sancerre Les Romains $35

Fine, silky, racy, and dry with notes of lime leaf, peach, Padrón pepper, white pepper, and chalk

Jean Reverdy La Reine Blanche, Sancerre $24

Light, delicate, and juicy with notes of white rose, yellow apple, and crushed sage along with its trademark chalky minerality

Pascal Jolivet Pouilly-Fumé $29

Brisk, dry, and tart with a creamy middle and notes of lime zest, peach, egg custard, and chalk

Vincent Vatan Pouilly-Fumé Selection Silex $22

Delicate, silky, crisp, and dry with notes of lime, peach, oregano, dill, white pepper, and chalk

Italy

Attems Sauvignon Blanc, Venezia Giulia $20

Light, crisp, and dry with notes of lemongrass, grapefruit, just-ripe peach, and sea salt

USA

Bernardus Sauvignon Blanc, Griva Vineyard, Arroyo Seco $24

Tangy and sweet-tart with notes of ripe cantaloupe, honeydew melon, peach, guava, star fruit, and fresh thyme

Dry Creek Vineyard DCV3 Estate Sauvignon Blanc, Dry Creek Valley $28

Fresh and juicy with notes of passion fruit, mango, papaya, lemongrass, bell pepper, jasmine, and honeysuckle

Matanzas Creek Sauvignon Blanc, Alexander Valley $20

Crisp, fresh, and dry with notes of lemon zest, peach, pineapple, and green bell pepper

St. Supéry Estate Sauvignon Blanc, Napa Valley $22

Lively, inviting, supple, and dry with notes of lime zest, pink grapefruit, green olive, fennel, and wildflowers

Trione Sauvignon Blanc, Russian River Valley $24

Rich and creamy with notes of Meyer lemon, lime zest, papaya, cantaloupe, honeysuckle, and nutmeg

New Zealand

Astrolabe Sauvignon Blanc, Marlborough $23

Warm, spicy, silky, and fresh with bold notes of peach and pear, red and green bell pepper, and dill

Cloudy Bay Te Koko Sauvignon Blanc, Marlborough $45

Rich, crisp, and dry with notes of lemongrass, peach, spring pea, asparagus, dried flowers, and hazelnut

Dog Point Sauvignon Blanc, Marlborough $24

Soft, delicate, dry, and fresh with notes of yellow apple, peach, apricot, cherimoya, spring pea, white pepper, wax, and honeysuckle

Greywacke Sauvignon Blanc, Marlborough $27

Fresh, lively, dry, and supple with notes of lime zest, lemongrass, chive, spring pea, dried sage, and chalk

Whitehaven Sauvignon Blanc, Marlborough $20

Mellow and fruity with notes of peach, pineapple, guava, mango, green bell pepper, and sage

Ata Rangi Sauvignon Blanc, Martinborough $22

Juicy, zippy, chalky, and clean with notes of green apple, apple butter, pear, pineapple, dill, wax, and black pepper

Craggy Range Sauvignon Blanc Te Muna Road, Martinborough $28

Lively and fresh with notes of lime zest, tangerine, Creamsicle, and fennel

Te Mata Cape Crest Sauvignon Blanc, Hawke's Bay $20

Barrel-aged and complex, a cellar-worthy Sauvignon Blanc with a little Sémillon and Sauvignon Gris

CALIFORNIA SAUVIGNON BLANC

America's premier wine growing district, California, enjoys its hard-earned reputation for Cabernet Sauvignon. But Sauvignon Blanc is equally at home there. Within California, the spectrum of microclimates runs from cool to hot, and Sauvignon Blanc ripens well in many of them. Winemakers often have a specific style in mind, or are tasked with it, to cater to a particular audience, or even to the tastes of a spouse.

Stylistically, California Sauvignon Blancs fall into three general categories: traditional, new wave, and modern. Producers of California Sauvignon Blanc initially looked to barrel-aged Chardonnay as a role model. Early offerings were rich, round, and fruity with an emphasis on melon and stone fruit (e.g., apricot or peach), and were lavishly oaky. They are rich, classy, understated, beautifully balanced, and expensive. The wildly successful New Zealand model—a vibrant interplay of ripe tropical and tart, grassy green notes, like that produced at St. Supéry, is the new wave. Folks love the vivacious flavors, the bright, ripe, refreshing rainbow in a glass. While this loud style works for some, it may not be for everyone. A modern style has evolved over the past few years that is light, crisp, and unoaked. This lively, clean, citrusy style plays down the green notes and goes for a more elegant expression of the grape.

One of California's earliest success stories with Sauvignon Blanc was the 1884 Cresta Blanca from Livermore Valley—a wide spot in a long chain of identical valleys running north–south behind the East Bay across the bay from San Francisco, and the warmest valley from the Bay area to Monterey. Charles Wetmore planted his Cresta Blanca vineyard in 1882 with cuttings of Sauvignon Blanc and Sémillon from Château d'Yquem in Bordeaux, France. This wine went on to win the Grand Prize at the 1889 Paris Expo, becoming the first American wine ever to win a prize in France. More recently, Hugh Johnson wrote about what a prime spot this valley is for Sauvignon Blanc due to its well-drained, gravelly limestone soil, similar to what is found in Bordeaux. The gravel, generally egg-size stones deposited by rushing waters that once ran through now-dry arroyos, are easily visible. Along Tesla Road, they can be as large as a melon or a basketball.

WORTH THE SPLURGE/SHOPPING $50 AND ABOVE

USA

Robert Mondavi Winery Fumé Blanc To Kalon Vineyard I Block, Oakville, Napa
  Valley $80

*Rich and creamy with notes of green apple, Asian pear, dried mango, musk, yellow rose,
banana pudding, wax, vanilla bean, almond, pecan, and cedar*

New Zealand

Giesen The Fuder Sauvignon Blanc Matthews Lane, Marlborough $50

*Aged in German oak Fuders (beer barrels), which softens and tones down signature
brassiness and adds creamy texture that showcases notes of thyme, sage, pear, and
melon*

LOIRE VALLEY SAUVIGNON BLANC

Known as "Le Jardin de la France," or France's garden, the Loire Valley is a
producer of wines enjoyed often and everywhere around the globe. As the
cradle of French civilization, the area has long attracted nobility. French
kings built summertime châteaus and hunting lodges in the sixteenth and
seventeenth centuries, bringing their household staffs along, including
sommeliers and chefs. The wines, as well as Marie-Antoine Carême, the
world's first celebrity chef, were discovered here.

Today the region is France's fourth-most-visited and its largest white-
wine producing region. Much of that is Sancerre, the dry, crisp, racy wine
enjoyed at the start of the meal as an aperitif, or "opener" of the appetite.
Sauvignon Blanc thrives in the Upper Loire, but the wine was not considered great until Sancerre and Pouilly-Fumé were discovered in nearby
Paris, and in America, in the 1960s.

While not a diva, cool-climate Sauvignon Blanc, especially when less
ripe, is pungent, herbaceous, even savage—*sauvage* in French is "wild,"
and in the case of the grape, unruly and productive. When reined in and
just ripe enough, however, the resulting wines offer the epitome of French
elegance. Didier Dagueneau was a local, very passionate renegade, whose
Pur Sang (*pur sang* means "purebred") was a game changer for the grape.
It is pricey and rare but worth seeking out, especially if someone else is
paying.

DINING OUT

The best way to tackle Sauvignon Blanc on a wine menu is by looking at the five areas where we find the world's best Sauvignon Blanc: France and Italy for Old World and USA, Chile, and New Zealand for New World. First, ask yourself whether you prefer the more restrained, understated, lean, and tart Old World style. If so, look to Sancerre and Pouilly-Fumé from France, and wines from Italy and Chile. Do you prefer the zesty, lively, and perhaps tropical style? Look to New Zealand. The variety of styles from California make selecting one in your preferred style difficult unless you know the producer, so it will be best to engage the sommelier or person who put together the wine list for advice.

Keep in mind when perusing the selections to look for only the most recent vintages. A safe window to stay in is one to three years.

THE GREAT FEAST OF THE WHITE ASPARAGUS

I am 21, an au pair living in a *chambre de bonne*, or maid's room, with a family on the rue de Babylone in Paris, and have been invited to dine with the family.

So we sit, and I notice different plates than usual. We each have before us a plate with a built-in wedge, as if put there to hold something up. We have a weird fork I had never seen before, even in the books at the library at hotel school—and I looked at a lot of forks, even got to know what some of them were for. Within seconds, we are entranced, spellbound, as the housekeeper serves us one by one with great reverence, as if she holds the firstborn son of a king in her hands. She rests the tender white spears gently on the wedge of the plate, so that they sit like a seesaw tip end up. She then circles us again, offering a sauce only the French could have created— so light and delicate yet so buttery and rich—which she drizzles gently over each spear. The room is silent. Madame looks at Monsieur, they nod, and we begin to eat. With this feast—the great feast of the white asparagus—we are served a delicate, slightly herbaceous Sancerre. The white asparagus was sublime, delicate, earthy, soft, delectable. The wine was perfect. It was in the background playing a supporting role, not the star of the show, its crispness perfectly cleansing the palate of any luxurious remnants of that silky sauce.

BRANCH OUT

VERDEJO

Spain's Rueda district is known for crisp, dry whites from the Verdejo grape blended with a little Viura and a little Sauvignon Blanc. These are not as grassy or pungent as Sauvignon Blanc.

Beronia Rueda, Spain $12

> *Crisp, light, zesty, and dry with notes of lime, green apple, banana, pineapple, leek, and spring pea*

GRÜNER VELTLINER

Austria's Grüner Veltliner has notes of white pepper and pink rose in addition to a light herbal streak.

Biokult Grüner Veltliner, Austria $14

> *Fresh, light, crisp, and dry with notes of lime, apricot, peach, white pepper, green bell and pasilla pepper, and chalk (organically grown)*

Check Your Success Quiz
1. What is the unique aroma/flavor of Sauvignon Blanc that is not typically found in other grapes?
2. Is Sauvignon Blanc considered refreshing or filling/satisfying?

3

CHARDONNAY

So popular, so beloved, and as comforting as Mom's apple pie, Chardonnay's charms are many. The world loves this friendly, happy, softly fruity, and approachable wine, a white with some heft to it. For the famous wine-producing Martinelli family of the Russian River Valley in California, this is the wine to drink with a breakfast of bacon and eggs, while sitting in a cool creek under the hot sun.

HISTORY

Chardonnay is one of the world's oldest grapes, believed to have descended from wild untamed vines that prefer to climb than produce fruit. Made popular during the medieval Crusades via transport through the Near and Middle East to Europe, it took hold particularly in France, officially birthed there as the offspring of Pinot Noir and Gouais Blanc. Chardonnay is the world's most popular white wine grape, and one that loses itself completely to winemaking techniques.

A Story of King Charlemagne and Why that Wine Is Now White

Charlemagne enjoyed his red wine, an elegant Pinot Noir from the hill of Corton. His wife thought he enjoyed it a little too much, often falling asleep glass in hand, causing it to run down his beard, onto his white shirt. Fed up, she forbade him from drinking red, which is why the wines known as Corton-Charlemagne are white, made with Chardonnay.

GEOGRAPHY

Chardonnay is easy to grow, and ripens early, allowing for successful results even in cooler locations. It produces wine with such richness and weight that when allowed to ripen fully in warmer locations, it can easily become flabby and unbalanced, lacking the freshness and focus provided by natural acidity.

While hugely successful in Burgundy and in Champagne, two famous growing regions in France, plantings in Australia, New Zealand, the Americas, and South Africa have given this grape a very high profile. Part of its success from these warmer, New World areas is that the word "Chardonnay" is actually on the front label, so you know what you are getting. Another part of the equation here is that the wines are crafted with the popular tastes, such as buttered popcorn and vanilla, in mind.

Thanks in part to its popularity, producers in every corner of the globe are jumping on the bandwagon. Sicily's Planeta and Donnafugata Chardonnays are so well received in the US markets that it gave them and other local producers a platform to introduce their native grapes here. In Greece, where indigenous grapes are also unique, plentiful, and full of local flavor, Chardonnay is produced not only for export, but for locals and tourists craving something international in style.

CHARDONNAY AT A GLANCE

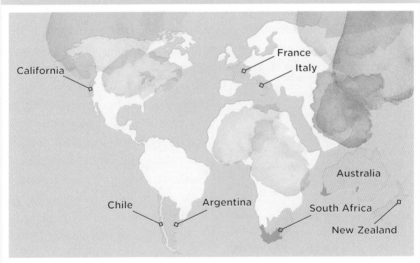

France: Burgundy, Champagne
Italy: Sicily
USA: California
Chile: Coastal Valleys
Argentina: Mendoza
South Africa: Western Cape
Australia: Margaret River, Barossa Valley
New Zealand

TASTE PROFILE AND STYLES

On its own, Chardonnay is shy with notes of citrus, apple, and pear. Chardonnay is made in a wide range of styles, with Burgundy, France, as its benchmark, where the region, not the grape, gives the wine its name. White Burgundy ranges from regional Bourgogne Blanc, whose quality is highly dependent upon the producer, to light, crisp Mâcon, to a steely, energetic Chablis, to nutty Meursault, and to very rich, layered, opulent, and complex Montrachet. It is the key ingredient in the ethereal, long-lived Blanc de Blancs Champagne from France, breathtaking in its purity, longevity, delicacy, and creaminess.

If the grape is picked just ripe, as in Chablis, Burgundy, and not manipulated in any way by the winemaker, it will produce the purest, most direct, and highest acid expression of Chardonnay. You will taste "naked" Chardonnay. In this case, along with a bit of subtle fruit, you might find an unusual taste of chalk, or oyster shell, taken in by the grape plant from the soil and ending up as a taste or, for some, a physical sensation on the tongue, like the feel of salt crystals.

If it is picked just ripe, again as in Chablis, Burgundy, then manipulated with either malolactic conversion or barrel fermentation and aging, or both, the acidity will be softened and the chalky taste may hide behind the shadow of the oak and butter. Farther south in Burgundy, fully ripe, luscious, and silky Chardonnays are produced in the villages of the Côte de Beaune, with the finest including Meursault (think of *somersault*, then say "mare-so") and Puligny-Montrachet ("poo-lee-nee mon-rash-ay"). (Think of Beaune as bone, and therefore white, as in Chardonnay. Montrachet is the name of the "bald mountain" near the village of Puligny).

Wines from the Mâconnais in southern Burgundy offer excellent value. Known as Mâcon and Mâcon-Villages (from villages that have

---

Winemaking vs. Grape Character

Malolactic conversion, which transforms tart malic acid to softer lactic acid (think: green apple to milk) makes the wine creamy and buttery. Richie Allen, Rombauer Vineyards' director of viticulture and winemaking, says, "Malolactic conversion is like the black magic of winemaking," explaining that malolactic conversion can be a difficult or frustrating thing for a winemaker to control. Some years it's very easy to get the wine through malo, whereas in others it can be very challenging. For Chardonnay, a lower percentage of malolactic conversion equates directly to less butter. Butter is a separate flavor than oak from the barrel.

Barrel fermentation and aging brings richness and roundness, and provides vanilla and baking spice notes, such as nutmeg, cinnamon, or clove.

vineyards just slightly better for growing and ripening Chardonnay), these are typically light and crisp with notes of white flowers, a pleasant chalky minerality (as in a high-mineral-count sparkling water—think Badoit or Gerolsteiner), and typically not oak or butter. Réserve des Rochers Mâcon-Chaintré is outstanding (Chaintré is the name of one of the villages).

Nearby Pouilly-Fuissé ("pwee fwee-say") is a source of rich, often oaky Chardonnays that can be overpriced, so shop carefully.

Bourgogne Blanc wines are regional blends, but if you do a little research or ask for expert advice, you will find such versions as the Olivier Leflaive Les Sétilles, which comes from high-quality vineyards in Meursault and Puligny-Montrachet.

In the warmer, New World regions of the world, the challenge in growing Chardonnay is to keep freshness and balance, as the grapes ripen so easily.

For the USA, the benchmark is California Chardonnay. Classically ripe, opulent, buttery, and oaky, they are as easygoing and satisfying as a sunny California day. At one extreme,

> **Pouilly-Fuissé vs. Pouilly-Fumé**
>
> "pwee fwee-say" vs. "pwee foo-may"
> That's easy for you to say! Seriously, what is the difference? Well, Pouilly-Fuissé is white Burgundy, which you now know is Chardonnay, and Pouilly-Fumé is Sauvignon Blanc from the Loire Valley, France (see page 48).

iconic brand Rombauer created the hugely popular "piña colada" style, which is still one of the most popular in restaurants and wine shops. Rombauer Chardonnay has a cultlike following, especially among ladies who lunch, and bee hunters, ladies on the prowl. If the Rombauer name sounds familiar for reasons other than its wines, look no further than *The Joy of Cooking*, written by Irma S. Rombauer, Marion Rombauer Becker, and Ethan Becker.

A bit lighter and less intense is the Sonoma-Cutrer Chardonnay, Russian River Valley, one of the most requested Chardonnays in US restaurants for 23 years, according to the *Wine & Spirits* Restaurant Poll.

A mass-market brand found everywhere that is truly well made and of great quality for the price is Kendall-Jackson Vintner's Reserve. This brand has been the number one best-selling Chardonnay in the country for 25 years, not only because of its price, but because of its style—a little butter, a little oak, and lemony freshness for balance. The original releases had musky florality from the addition of Muscat and other grapes but are now 100 percent Chardonnay. The quality is high, as the family-owned operation has vast resources, including vineyards, talented staff, and production facilities across the state.

In a past issue of the *Wine Spectator*, 33 out of 36 ninety-plus-point wines had a common adjective—"rich." Château Montelena owners Jim and Bo Barrett said, "We're gonna make a wine that is compatible with food and will improve with age, not a boozy Chardonnay."

A handful of Napa Valley wineries, including Robert Mondavi and Château Montelena, produce wines that are more subtle, understated, compatible with food, and capable of aging. The secret to aging is picking grapes early, when they are barely ripe and have high levels of natural acidity. Natural acid brings balance, freshness, focus, and longevity to wine.

The latest style craze in Chardonnay is the unoaked style. In particular, the UK and USA markets are crowded with unoaked versions, which are growing in popularity, as they are lighter and crisper. Mer Soleil Silver, from the Wagner family of Caymus fame, leads this category. These are on paper closer in style to unoaked Chablis from northern Burgundy but they are typically far riper and richer and much lower in natural acidity. In other words, they are still pleasantly plump and easy to enjoy as a cocktail.

From South America, there are rich, ripe Chardonnays from Mendoza, Argentina, and styles ranging from light and crisp to moderately ripe and lightly oaked

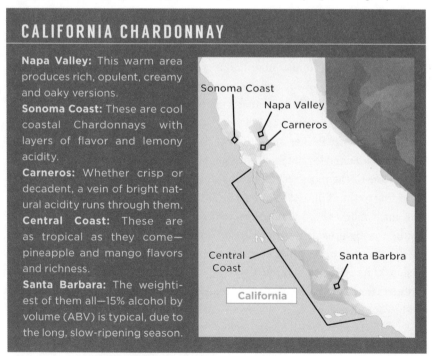

CALIFORNIA CHARDONNAY

Napa Valley: This warm area produces rich, opulent, creamy and oaky versions.

Sonoma Coast: These are cool coastal Chardonnays with layers of flavor and lemony acidity.

Carneros: Whether crisp or decadent, a vein of bright natural acidity runs through them.

Central Coast: These are as tropical as they come—pineapple and mango flavors and richness.

Santa Barbara: The weightiest of them all—15% alcohol by volume (ABV) is typical, due to the long, slow-ripening season.

Sonoma Coast

Napa Valley

Carneros

Central Coast

Santa Barbra

California

Ten Grapes to Know

Chardonnay is as smooth, easygoing, and upbeat as a Pharrell Williams song. It is memorable and comforting. There is enough to listen to, but it is also pleasant ambient sound.

CHARDONNAY DATING PROFILE

- I am rich and have great legs.
- I may be a lighter style, but I am still very satisfying.
- I am a chameleon, which keeps things interesting.
- I am not aromatic, and not very fruity, unless I'm from the California coast, man.
- I am not chewy or gripping, rather soft, silky, and smooth, like butter.
- Speaking of butter, I am often buttery, but not always.
- Sometimes I am golden in color, from time lounging in oak barrels. If I am golden, I am nutty, or taste like vanilla bean or caramel corn.
- If I am French, well, I am very different from my California cousins. Of course, I am more elegant, more refined, and I offer a glimpse into where I was raised.
- I am naked. That is, if I am from Chablis, and don't spend time in oak barrels.
- I will not stain your teeth.
- Or your clothing.

in Chile, the best of these from cool coastal valleys, such as Casablanca and Leyda. South Africa's Western Cape is an area to look for as well, with such producers as Neil Ellis in Elgin and De Wetshof in Robertson.

In Australia, as in California, the warmer the vineyard area, the riper the Chardonnay. Margaret River is a cool climate on the west coast. Leeuwin is a classic, long-standing producer of this lighter, crisper style. If you don't see Leeuwin, look for other brands from Margaret River. Barossa Valley Chardonnays, such as Hewitson, are a bit riper and fuller, as it is warmer there than in Margaret River.

From cool and brilliantly sunny New Zealand, there is a range of styles, but for

> **Cougar Juice**
>
> In California, I always hear sommeliers and retail wine buyers complain about big, buttery, oaky Chardonnays that can overpower a meal. They call them "Danville crack" or "cougar juice." They are, after all, safe for bleached teeth, and savvy young sommeliers know to offer to them.

the most part you will find nicely balanced bright wines with a little butter and oak. The style is not exaggerated in any way. One notable exception is the linear, crisp, incredibly mineral-laden Kumeu River Estate Chardonnay from the country's first Master of Wine, Michael Brajkovich. He is known there as the Master of Chardonnay.

MATCHMAKING

Lighter, crisper Chardonnays pair well with shellfish and delicate fish dishes, whereas riper, bolder Chardonnays taste delicious with lobster, crab, and chicken. Adding mushrooms connects to an earthy element in the French versions. Avoid spice and heat, which will overwhelm the lighter versions and clash with the richer wines. A bridge from a buttery Chardonnay to a buttery crab leg is one way to up your pairing game—dance from wine to bite and back seamlessly.

Chardonnay is easy to enjoy as a cocktail, especially if it is flavored with vanilla from oak and butter from malolactic conversion.

EVERY DAY WITH CHARDONNAY
Bacon and eggs

Corn chowder

Cobb salad

Fresh cracked crab

Seafood salad

Lobster roll

Sautéed halibut with pecan butter

Pork loin with cannellini beans

Buttermilk fried chicken

Pasta/rice/quinoa/farro with mushroom cream sauce

INSTA DINNER

Lean Cuisine—Chicken Ranch Club Flatbread Melt

Lean Cuisine—Glazed Turkey Tenderloins with Whipped Sweet Potatoes

Pizza bianca made with Trader Joe's fresh pizza dough, cheese, and mushrooms

UPSCALE CONVENIENCE

Home Chef—Skillet Chicken Chasseur with Mushrooms and White Wine (replace the
included 2 ounces of wine with the Chardonnay you are serving)

SNACK

Air-popped popcorn with drizzled real butter and sea salt (Maldon Salt is worth the
splurge and is available at Williams-Sonoma and Cost Plus)

DINNER TONIGHT

DIJON-CRUSTED CRISPY BAKED CHICKEN TENDERLOINS WITH SAUTÉED
MUSHROOMS

This guilt-free crunchy chicken, mustard tang, and earthy mushrooms pair well with the
silky, understated, and lemony white Burgundy, the Réserve des Rochers, Mâcon-Chaintré
$17, or the creamy and opulent yet fresh and tingly Wente Vineyards Chardonnay Riva
Ranch, Arroyo Seco $22.

SHOPPING

Like anything else, avoid the gimmicky labels like "buttered popcorn" or those
with a critter on them. The quality of California Roots, Target's new $5 private
label, is dependent on who is involved in sourcing and manufacturing. This is
something I do occasionally but not every company brings in a Master Sommelier. Try one and if you like it, go back for more.

Now this might come to some of you as a shocker, but I recommend the
Kendall-Jackson Vintner's Reserve as a go-to in a pinch, especially if you find
yourself staring at the wall of Chardonnay and don't know what to choose. This is
not something I would recommend for a wine list in a restaurant, but for a quick
grocery store pick, you can't go wrong.

While more than a million cases a year are produced, Kendall-Jackson's wines
all touch oak—not a problem for such a large-scale family-operated business—
and as the family owns and controls the vineyards, production, and distribution,
the quality is above par and the price value ratio is off the charts.

EVERYDAY VALUE/SHOPPING UNDER $20

France
Réserve des Rochers, Mâcon-Chaintré $17
   Crisp, silky, and subtle with notes of lemon peel, lemon leaf, chalk, and coriander

USA
Barefoot Chardonnay, California $6
   Soft, inviting, and sweet-tart with notes of apple pie, grilled pineapple, and cinnamon toast
Kendall-Jackson Vintner's Reserve Chardonnay, California $17
   Creamy, soft, and dry with notes of lemon curd, banana pudding, peach, pineapple, buttered toast, and walnut

Chile
Santa Rita Chardonnay Gran Reserva Medalla Real, Leyda Valley $18
   Creamy and delicate with notes of apple pie, white cherry, grilled peach, and butter

Argentina
Portillo Chardonnay, Mendoza $10
   Soft and creamy with notes of lemon, apple, ginger cookie, and butterscotch

South Africa
De Wetshof Chardonnay Unwooded Limestone Ridge, Robertson $16
   Creamy and fresh with notes of lemon curd, apple butter, and vanilla ice cream

New Zealand
Esk Valley Chardonnay, Hawke's Bay $16
   Silky, fresh, delicate, and dry with notes of apple, peach, almond butter, nutmeg, and chalk
Glazebrook Regional Reserve Chardonnay, Hawke's Bay $16
   Lemony, delicate, and very silky with notes of Gala apple, butter cookie, walnut, cinnamon, and white chocolate

IMPRESS YOUR GUESTS/SHOPPING $20-$50

France

Domaine Laroche, Chablis Saint Martin $26

Silky, then bracingly dry and tart with notes of lemon crème, freshly whipped cream, oyster shell, and crème brûlée

Olivier Leflaive, Bourgogne Blanc Les Sétilles $28

Delicate, clean, fresh, and tangy with notes of lemon zest, vanilla custard, crème fraîche, and sea salt

Matrot, Bourgogne Chardonnay $26

Soft and tingly with notes of apple tart, butter cookie, and crème fraîche

J.J. Vincent, Pouilly-Fuissé Marie Antoinette $29

Silky and tart with notes of lemon zest, red apple, vanilla bean, and toasted pecan

Château Fuissé, Pouilly-Fuissé $24

Smooth, smoky, chalky, and elegant

Italy

Donnafugata Chardonnay Chiaranda, Contessa Entellina $40

Soft and fresh with notes of lemon, apricot, pineapple, and almond croissant

Planeta Chardonnay, Menfi $42

Full, dry, and lightly spiced with notes of lemon custard, tangerine, sea salt, butter, and nutmeg

USA

Artesa Chardonnay, Los Carneros, Sonoma $20

Fresh, silky, and dry with notes of lemon, cantaloupe, banana, vanilla, chamomile, lanolin, and sea spray

Duckhorn Vineyards Chardonnay, Napa Valley $35

Soft and silky with notes of lemon butter, apple pie, papaya, buttered toast, and ginger

La Crema Chardonnay, Sonoma Coast $23

Creamy and fresh with notes of lemon zest, pear, peach, kiwi, and buttered toast

Martinelli Chardonnay Bella Vigna, Sonoma Coast $45

Soft, round, and full with notes of peaches and cream, buttered toast, and vanilla bean

Rombauer Vineyards Chardonnay, Carneros $38

Ripe and opulent with notes of peach, pineapple, butterscotch, caramel corn, and coconut

Sonoma-Cutrer Chardonnay Russian River Ranches, Sonoma Coast $28

Full, rich, and bright with notes of white apricot, peach, lemon meringue, butterscotch, and pecan

Wente Vineyards Chardonnay Riva Ranch, Arroyo Seco $22

Creamy and opulent while fresh and tingly with notes of green apple, pear, vanilla custard, butter, and walnut

Schramsberg Blanc de Blancs Brut, North Coast $39

Elegant with a fine, long-lasting effervescence and notes of lemon zest, apricot, crème brûlée, and white rose

Australia

Hewitson Chardonnay Miss Harry, Barossa Valley $20

Creamy and silky with a tart lemon undercurrent and notes of peach pie, crème fraîche, brioche, and almond

Leeuwin Estate Chardonnay Prelude Vineyards, Margaret River $40

Soft, layered, beautifully balanced, and long with notes of pithy white peach, Bosc pear, unsalted butter, white rose, and sage

New Zealand

Kumeu Village Chardonnay Kumeu, Hawke's Bay $22

Lean, racy, and tangy with notes of lime zest, white peach, sea salt, and baguette

WORTH THE SPLURGE/SHOPPING $50 AND ABOVE

France

Olivier Leflaive, Meursault $60

Fresh, dry, silky, and subtle with notes of lemon curd, grilled pineapple, white mushroom, and chalk

Olivier Leflaive, Puligny-Montrachet $80

Delicate, silky, and fresh with notes of peach, almond, caramel apple, and chalk

Delamotte Blanc de Blancs Brut, Le Mesnil-sur-Oger, Champagne $90

This classy bubbly beauty is pure chalky and refined Chardonnay at its best—it is known in the trade as "Baby Salon"

Gosset Grand Blanc de Blancs Brut, Champagne $92

Fine and delicate with white flowers, chalk, and almond croissant

USA

Château Montelena Chardonnay, Napa
  Valley $58

  *Complex, silky, tart, and dry with
  notes of lemon zest, peach, apple tart,
  ginger, cashew, and caramel*

Iron Horse Ocean Reserve Blanc de
  Blancs Brut, Green Valley of Russian
  River Valley $50

  *Zesty and refined with notes of rising
  bread, lemon tart, and apple pie*

French Wine Names

French wines have sexy, sophisticated-sounding names, such as Bienvenue-Bâtard-Montrachet and Pisse-Vieille, but if you look more closely, you discover that these names mean, "Welcome, bastard, to the bald mountain" and "Pee already, old woman!"

Australia

Leeuwin Estate Chardonnay Art Series, Margaret River $80

  *Very silky, elegant, and tangy with notes of lemon zest, mandarin, peach, butter cookie,
  and hazelnut*

CHAMPAGNE

Champagne is produced in an old province 90 miles northeast of Paris, France. Champagne may be exclusively Chardonnay (Blanc de Blancs) or Pinot Noir and/or Pinot Meunier (Blanc de Noirs)— or a blend of all three grapes. Chardonnay represents 30 percent of total vines planted in the official growing area of Champagne.

Champagnes range in style from multi-vintage blends, known as non-vintage (NV), to pricier vintage Champagnes from the fruit of one specific year, and from Brut (or dry), to Extra Dry (barely sweet), Sec (sweet), and Doux (dessert sweet).

Champagne production involves highly skilled artisans working in the vineyards and cellar, overseeing the quality of the grapes and shepherding them as they transform into the most famous sparkling wine in the world. What separates these high-quality bubblies from others is a second fermentation in bottle. This step allows for the development of those flavors we love, such as crème brûlée, and for a very fine bead (tiny bubbles).

Why drink Champagne?
The wire muzzle makes a great cat toy.

DINING OUT

In more casual establishments that don't have a sommelier or wine buyer on the floor, refer to my list of recommended wines. Open the wine list, find the Chardonnays from the New World, and look for wines from specific regions, such as Carneros, Sonoma Coast, or Arroyo Seco. Then, go to France and scan for Chablis, Meursault, Montrachet, Pouilly-Fuissé, and Mâcon. Do engage the sommelier if there is one, and give them an idea of what style or brand you tend to order, and a price range.

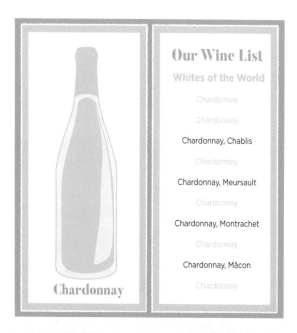

Chardonnay

Our Wine List

Whites of the World

Chardonnay

Chardonnay

Chardonnay, Chablis

Chardonnay

Chardonnay, Meursault

Chardonnay

Chardonnay, Montrachet

Chardonnay

Chardonnay, Mâcon

Chardonnay

CHARDONNAY AS A COCKTAIL

Napa Valley producer Rombauer sells 175,000 cases a year of what is considered the quintessential California Chardonnay, the Rombauer Vineyards Chardonnay Carneros $38. It tastes like a piña colada and that is what makes it so popular. Rombauer also produces a serious lineup of vineyard-specific Chardonnays that show off their origin more than style but hardly anyone knows about those. One to look for is the lush, round, and bright Rombauer Vineyards Chardonnay Home Ranch, Carneros $70.

Ten Grapes to Know

BRANCH OUT

PINOT BLANC

Pinot Blancs are broad and creamy if not oaky and buttery, and you will love the prices.

Pierre Sparr Pinot Blanc, Alsace $17
Light and fresh with notes of Meyer lemon, Gala apple, honeycomb, and almond slivers
Dutton Goldfield Pinot Blanc Shop Block Dutton Ranch, Green Valley of Russian River Valley $30
Crisp, clean, and silky with notes of yellow apple, hazelnut, almond croissant, and pound cake

---

Check Your Success Quiz

1. The rich, ripe, buttery, and oaked style of California Chardonnay pairs nicely with the most delicate of fish dishes. True/False
2. Mâcon and Meursault are two areas in Burgundy, France, where the grape is Chardonnay. True/False

---

VIOGNIER

grape goddess says:
"Vee-ohn-yay." Repeat after me: "Vee-ohn-yay."

For many, this grape is a challenge to pronounce. For farmers, it is a challenge to cultivate. So why is it even around? Quite simply, the wine is devilishly seductive and intoxicating.

I've heard folks ask for "we-ahg-ner," "vee-ohn-nee-yay," "von-yee-ay," and so on. Being hard to pronounce is a common reason folks will skip a new wine and just ask for one they already are familiar with.

HISTORY

Legend has it that in AD 281 Emperor Probus brought Viognier grapes from Dalmatia (present-day Croatia) to France and planted them into the steep, terraced hillsides of Condrieu on the west bank of the Rhône River near the city of Vienne. Vines had been growing there during the Roman occupation but one of Probus's predecessors, Emperor Vespasian, had ripped them out. According to the owners of Château Grillet, the most famous producer of Condrieu, historical records confirm the grape was grown here during the Roman Empire.

In the 1920s, more than 370 acres were planted there, but with the labor involved in working the steep, terraced vineyards and the low yield of fruit, many were abandoned. In 1940, Condrieu become an official French wine appellation, but the plantings of Viognier dwindled and nearly disappeared. Condrieu pioneer and visionary Georges Vernay, who took over his family winery in 1953, saved the day by convincing growers to keep Viognier in the ground, not abandon it for other crops.

From the late 1980s and throughout the '90s, Rhône wines enjoyed something of a renaissance. Demand for Syrah and Viognier was on the rise and many neglected vineyards were reinvigorated. American wine lovers followed the rise of the Rhône Rangers, pioneering California winemakers such as Randall Grahm of Bonny Doon Vineyard in Santa Cruz and Josh Jensen of Calera Wine Company in San Benito County near Monterey, who wanted to plant something other than the ubiquitous Chardonnay and Cabernet Sauvignon.

GEOGRAPHY

Today Viognier is widely planted in the northern Rhône's Condrieu, including at Château Grillet, one of France's smallest appellations, with less than 10 acres and only one owner. Château Grillet is a "nested" or subappellation within Condrieu itself.

There are a handful of plantings in Côte-Rôtie to the north, where appellation rules allow up to 20 percent Viognier added to the Syrah. This law was written to give winemakers a chance to produce a richer, rounder Syrah in weaker years, just as in Bordeaux, where Cabernet Sauvignon is rounded out as needed with Merlot and other grapes. With unfavorable weather, the team player approach is a must. But in practice, most winemakers would frown upon diluting their red Syrah with the white Viognier. Since the law was written, clonal research and the return to natural farming has provided much cleaner, healthier fruit year after year.

After Georges Duboeuf planted large swathes of land in the Ardèche in south-central France with Viognier, folks in the neighboring Languedoc regions began planting it as well. Today varietally labeled Vin de Pays wines are very popular and not too pricey. There are several new producers in South West France as well.

In the New World, aside from plantings in California, where they are most often found in the Central Coast, there are plantings in Chile, Australia, and even Brazil.

Sensitive Viognier is prone to mildew in damp or humid conditions. It produces a very small crop. If it is not picked fully ripe, it won't offer its trademark perfume of peaches and white flowers. If it is picked too ripe, it will be flabby, as the grape is naturally low in acidity.

DOMAINE GEORGES VERNAY

Legendary producer Georges Vernay, who saved Viognier from going extinct in the 1960s, passed away early in 2017. His daughter Christine, representing the winery's third generation, runs the winery today with her husband, Paul Amsellem. Georges embraced the history of the area, naming one vineyard "Terrasses de l'Empire," referring to the steep, terraced hillside vineyards planted by the Romans. Christine and Paul, both lovers of jazz and classical music, bring people together around wine and music through a major biannual event held at the estate, with international artists.

France

Ardèche

Northern Rhône

South West France

Languedoc

France:

- Northern Rhône: Condrieu
- Ardèche
- Languedoc
- South West
- Vin de Pays

USA:

- California: Central Coast

Chile

TASTE PROFILES AND STYLES

Imagine getting off the plane in the tropics—sweet perfumed air, white sand, hot sun, azure sea, and lazy days ahead. With floral, apricot, honeyed, and tropical notes, Viognier is a sultry temptress.

In its best expression, the wine is as fat and silky on the midpalate as white Burgundy, or French Chardonnay, and shares the same minerality. The difference is the delicate floral aromas and ripe apricot flavors rather than classic white Burgundy's crème brûlée and butterscotch. There is nothing quite like the decadent enjoyment of a floral, exotic, honeyed Condrieu with a handful of ripe apricots. Old World, or French, Viogniers are dry and rich with subtle fruit and perfume, noticeable minerality, and, in a turn from the norm, low to medium acidity.

Viognier in the New World, particularly in California, such as Napa Valley's Joseph Phelps Vineyards and Josh Jensen's Calera Wine Company, are more intense and fruitier than French versions. The wines are high in alcohol, low in acidity, and dry. Late-harvest, sweet versions are rare but delicious.

The popularity of Viognier can be attributed to its unique flavor profile—peach, apricot, mango, white flowers, and honey; the sumptuousness of Chardonnay without the butter; and a softness and plushness not found in zingy, zesty Sauvignon Blanc.

Oz Clarke says in his book written with Margaret Rand, *Grapes & Wines*, "If you wanted serious, swooning wine, with texture as soft and thick as apricot juice, perfume as optimistic and uplifting as mayblossom, and a savoury sour creamy richness like a dollop of crème fraiche straight from the ladle of a farmer's wife—in other words, a wine which just oozed sex and sensuality—Condrieu, from the Viognier grape, was it."

MUSICIAN

 Rich, heady, luxurious, and rare, the voice of sultry jazz singer Diana Krall is like no other.

DATING PROFILE

- I am forthright, adventurous, young at heart, and enthusiastic.
- I am rich and distinctive with a soft side.
- I am highly perfumed—intoxicating, even.
- My charms are fleeting so enjoy them before it is too late.
- Show me off. I am great arm candy.

MATCHMAKING

Viognier has classic and specific fruit tones of ripe apricot, floral notes of honeysuckle, high alcohol, and low acidity. In other words, it is more of a scene-stealing diva than a pairing partner.

However, certain pairings, when engineered with just a little thought, are spectacular. Employing the technique of mirroring is helpful here, as in adding apricot to the dish as a flavor bridge to the wine. Avoid heat or heavy spice. Those elements need either a little sweetness or a lot of acidity to cool off and refresh the palate.

The creaminess and pleasant fruitiness of Viognier is a nice pairing with milder cheeses from soft to gently firm in texture.

EVERY DAY WITH VIOGNIER
Grilled prawns and peaches
Lobster roll (substitute crab or crab sticks/*kamaboko*)
Fish taco with mango, cilantro, corn, and corn tortilla
Baked cod with peaches and lemon oil
Apricot-lemon pork or veal chops
Quinoa with dried apricot and toasted pecan

INSTA DINNER
Lean Cuisine—Chicken Pecan
Lean Cuisine—Roasted Turkey Breast
Frozen orange chicken

UPSCALE CONVENIENCE
Hello Fresh—Honey-Roasted Squash with Warm Mushroom and Quinoa Salad

SNACK
Cheese with crackers and dried apricots

CHEESE
Laughing Cow spreadable wedges
Babybel
Gruyère de Comte
Port Salut

DINNER TONIGHT

GROCERY-STORE ROASTED CHICKEN WITH APRICOT RICE

Microwave a little apricot jam and water and pour over rice or other grain and garnish with slivered almonds. Serve with the chicken and the fresh, delicate, and dry Jean Luc Colombo Viognier La Violette, Vin de Pays d'Oc $14, or the organically-farmed fresh and tangy Bonterra Viognier, Mendocino $16.

VIOGNIER AND OAK

One year at the Hospice du Rhône in Paso Robles, California, a celebration of Rhône wines, I approached the quite attractive Michel Chapoutier, who had captured the hearts of so many of my female colleagues. As a newly minted Master Sommelier, I thought I was a hotshot. It wore off quickly—I was complaining about how oaky the Rosenblum Viognier Contra Costa County was, just like our overoaked California Chardonnays. I praised him and the French in general for not ruining their Viognier with oak. Michel then proceeded to explain to me how his family's wines, including the Condrieu, spend at least two years in new French oak barrels.

SHOPPING

EVERYDAY VALUE/SHOPPING UNDER $20

France

Domaine des Cantarelles Viognier, Vin de Pays du Gard $14

> *Very perfumed, fruity, and soft with notes of lily, jasmine, freesia, ripe apricot, white peach, chalk, and citrus*

Jean-Luc Colombo Viognier La Violette, Vin de Pays d'Oc $14

> *Fresh, delicate, and dry with notes of apricot, peach, yellow rose, and tuberose*

USA

Calera Viognier, Central Coast $18

> *Round and juicy with notes of pineapple, mango, jasmine, peach pit, almond, and hazelnut*

Bonterra Viognier, Mendocino $16

> *Full, fresh, and tangy with notes of lemon, apricot, peach, and mango (organically farmed)*

Parducci Small Lot Viognier, Mendocino $15

> *Full and lusciously fruity with notes of tangerine, canned peach, pineapple, mango, and white rose*

Steele Viognier, Lake County $19

> *Bright and lively with notes of peach, mango, sweet-tart lemon drop, and mint*

Chile

Cono Sur Bicicleta Viognier, Chile $12

Juicy and crisp with notes of ripe peach, mango, white rose, chamomile tea, and lemon zest

IMPRESS YOUR GUESTS/SHOPPING $20-$50

France

Château Lagrézette Viognier Mas de Merveilles Rocamadour, Côtes du Lot, South West France $35

Dry, pithy, elegant, and soft with notes of peach pit, apricot, rose petal, talc, and lemon zest

Domaine Georges Vernay Viognier Le Pied de Samson, Vin de Pays Collines Rhodaniennes $32

Light, silky, dry, and fresh with notes of peach, apricot, white rose, talc, and sea salt

USA

Alban Winery Viognier, Central Coast $26

Soft and inviting with notes of pear, peach, pineapple and caramel

Eberle Winery Viognier Mill Road Vineyard, Paso Robles $26

Silky, supple, and plush with notes of lemon, peach, chamomile buds, and hazelnut

WORTH THE SPLURGE/SHOPPING $50 AND ABOVE

France

Château Lagrezette Viognier Le Pigeonnier White Vision, Côtes du Lot, South West France $90

Full, silky, layered, and complex with notes of apple, pear, peach, dried pineapple, white rose, chalk, and sea spray

Domaine Georges Vernay, Condrieu Terrasses de L'Empire $90

Silky and dry with chalky minerality, lemony freshness, and notes of peach, pear, and chamomile buds

Vidal-Fleury, Condrieu $78

Silky, dry, and delicate with notes of mango, pineapple, lily, lilac, chalk, ginger, and flan

Yves Cuilleron, Condrieu La Petite Côte $50

Classic Viognier silk and vibrancy framed by pith and tartness and notes of clementine, apricot, ginger, and saffron

DINING OUT

On a visit to the Rhône Valley with a French sommelier I was dating, we visited a restaurant on the river in the village of Condrieu. Naturally, it had an extensive wine list with Condrieus going back more than 20 vintages. I had never seen such a collection and was anxious to try an older wine. I had learned already not to buy older vintages, as with low natural acidity, the wines become flabby and oxidative fairly early in their lives. But I figured here in Condrieu, the locals knew best. Boy, was I wrong. We tried one oxidized bottle after another until I final told Henri to stop. Lesson learned. Drink fresh recent vintages only.

When deciding which Viognier to order, aside from looking for vintages only one to three years old, engage the sommelier or server or ask for the "wine person" if the establishment has one, and get his or her two cents. If such people have selected the wines for the list, they can tell you firsthand their stories and why they are excited about them. Otherwise, use my recommended wines as a guide and remember that the French versions are lighter and relatively subtle, while the California wines will have much more of a fruit pop.

SENSE EXERCISE

Blind Tasting White Wine

Now that you have reached the fourth and final white grape section, let's see how your palate has progressed. Take a bottle or glass of one of my recommended Viogniers and place it side by side with either a Sauvignon Blanc, Chardonnay, or Pinot Gris. Have a partner or friend keep track of which is which, and taste them blind, not knowing the order. How did you do?

JOSH JENSEN—CALERA

The following is excerpted from my interview with Josh Jensen, Calera Wine Company, Mount Harlan, California, in the Sommelier Journal, *July 2009.*

Calera had been on my radar from the earliest days of my wine education. I had read about it in the textbooks for Harriet Lembeck's wine course, a prerequisite for my job at Windows on the World in New York City. When Kevin Zraly finally hired me there, I found several Calera wines on his carefully crafted list, and by then I knew that any winery with multiple listings was to be held in the highest regard. That was in 1989. Ten years and a Master Sommelier certificate later, I found myself face to face with the man behind the winery, Josh Jensen, interviewing him for the *Global Encyclopedia of Wine* in a trailer at his remote winery in the Gabilan Mountains. Even then I felt a bit intimidated. Here I was, meeting the Oxford-educated, French-speaking, and very precise man whose Pinot Noirs and Viogniers had been recognized as the equals of their French counterparts. Here I was, tasting his great single-vineyard Pinots, young and old, and later, bouncing around in a four-wheel-drive truck at the top of a mountain, in the rugged vineyards the world now knows as the Mount Harlan American Viticultural Area. Jensen is formal, and his wines are formidable.

It came as something of a shock, a few years after that, when I was well ensconced in the San Francisco hospitality scene, to find Jensen pulling up at midnight or so in front of the Globe—the favored late-night hangout of front-and-back-of-the-house workers from all over the city. Here he was, Mr. Limestone, the icon, the Pinot god himself, unfolding his long limbs and stepping out of a tiny red sports coupe, flashing a brightly colored leather biker jacket and sporting a couple of magnums of his wine. It was going to be a very good night.

In 2009, I met with Jensen at his beautiful new winery, built on the same spot where we had conducted our first interview in a trailer.

CF: *So from Oxford you went to France looking for harvest work?*
JJ: Yes, I just knocked on the front door of Domaine de la Romaneé-Conti at the start of the 1970 harvest season. There was this tough old bird there who was the office manager, Mademoiselle Clin. Everybody was afraid of her. She eyed me up and down and said, "Well, I guess you look like you could do the work," and she said, "We start in a week. Come back in a week." I hustled on down to Château-Grillet, next door to Condrieu—because I had also talked to them about picking there—and they said, "We start tomorrow morning." So I drove right down in my little Citroën 2CV Camionette and did the two-day harvest down at Grillet. That was actually the first winery I ever worked in, and I told them that instead of being paid in money, I wanted to be paid in bottles of Château-Grillet. So for the two long days' work, I got three bottles.

BRANCH OUT

RIESLING AND TORRONTÉS

Sometimes Viognier is mistaken for Riesling in a blind tasting. Both these grapes are highly aromatic, as is Torrontés from Argentina.

Familia Zuccardi Torrontés, Argentina $15
> *Vibrant, fresh, and supple with notes of lemon, pineapple, banana, and jasmine*

Pacific Rim J Riesling, Columbia Valley $11
> *Lightly sweet and creamy with notes of lime zest, Golden Delicious apple, Bosc pear, peach, and cotton candy*

Check Your Success Quiz

1. Pairing spicy foods with wines high in alcohol and low in acidity will yield good results. True/False
2. An ideal addition to a Viognier pairing is
   (a) Ancho chile
   (b) Garlic
   (c) Apricot
   (d) Bacon

5

PINOT NOIR

grape goddess says:
"Peeno nwaahr." Repeat after me: "Peeno nwaahr."

Pinot Noir is the lightest of all reds. With enticing notes of raspberry, cranberry, rose petal, mushroom, and exotic spice, Pinot Noir is a favorite of sommeliers, winemakers, and romantics. It is delicately perfumed and often tart, but don't let that fool you. This one can hit all the high notes and sustain your interest over a lifetime. Why? This noble red grape makes an intensely flavored, complex, high-acid wine with incredible longevity. As the climate where it is grown gets warmer, the fruit becomes riper and more obvious, and the acid softens a bit. The net result in any case is a wine that will not overpower your meal.

Winemakers love this grape because it is so temperamental. They try to tame it and master it, but they cannot. It is impetuous and does what it wants. But when it is good, it is really good. Sommeliers love it because it beautifully showcases even the most ethereal dishes. It just brings so much joy! Somms love to geek out on Burgundy, or French Pinot Noir. We taste it, add it to our wine lists, sell it to our guests, buy it for our cellars (or makeshift cellars), and bring it out when we get together. It is the ultimate beverage and a lifelong passion.

Pinot Noir along with Pinot Gris and Pinot Blanc are referred to as the Pinot family, and it is considered a distant cousin of Syrah.

HISTORY

Pinot Noir is one of the oldest grapes on the planet, a direct descendant from wild vines and one of the first cultivated specifically for wine. Romans found it already growing in Burgundy when they arrived over 2,000 years ago, and by 1395, Pinot Noir had become the signature grape of the region. Early and notable success both in Burgundy and farther north in Champagne as an elegant rosé sparkling wine gave rise to its popularity and growth around the world.

GEOGRAPHY

From the subtle, delicate Chambolle-Musigny to the exotic Richebourg, Pinot Noirs from the bucolic hillside areas of France collectively known as Burgundy are the role models for the world. No other grape delivers a wine with such heady perfume, silky texture, and primal, earthy flavor.

Within Burgundy, the Côte d'Or, made up of the Côte de Nuits and the Côte de

Beaune, is home to a string of villages producing tiny lots of Pinot Noirs named by their place of origin—in this case, village or ranked vineyard. *Côte* means "hillside," and the best vineyards, those with the highest rankings, which in this case are Grand Cru, are midslope. Premier Cru is one step down, and below that is simply the larger "village," then even larger regional name level. While Pinot Noir is grown in both the Côte de Nuits, or "hillside of night," and the Côte de Beaune, or "hillside of Beaune," the best come from Côte de Nuit. Think black grapes from night, white (Chardonnay) from bone.

Because there are multiple owners of these vineyards, it is very important to become familiar with the style and quality of the producer. The use of a famous Grand Cru name doesn't always translate to a fabulous bottle of Pinot Noir, and you can be sure this will be a costly disappointment.

Use this list as a handy reference of villages when making your selection. It will give you an idea of where the wine is from:

Côte d'Or
  Côte de Nuits
    Gevrey-Chambertin
    Morey-St-Denis
    Chambolle-Musigny
    Vougeot
    Vosne-Romanée
    Nuits-St-Georges

Most of these villages have Grand Cru vineyards, often the name that has been hyphenated to the original village name. So the Grand Crus of Gevrey-Chambertin have "Chambertin" in their name. The Grand Cru of Chambolle-Musigny is, you guessed it, Musigny. (One exception is Nuits-St-Georges.)

Wines from areas larger than a single vineyard or small village, such as Mercurey in the Côte Chalonnaise to the south or Hautes-Côtes de Nuits within the Côte de Nuits, are sources of good quality and nicely priced Pinot Noirs. The largest regional appellation in Burgundy is Bourgogne. Bourgogne Rouge or even Bourgogne Pinot Noir would be on the label.

The other great French Pinot Noir is Rosé Champagne. Pinot Noir–dominated Champagne, fuller and fruiter than Chardonnay, and often rosé or salmon colored, is considered the most serious. While most Champagne is a blend, Bollinger, Krug, and other top names produce exquisite interpretations of Pinot Noir that are rich, powerful, and long-lived.

Crémant is France's required name for Champagne-method sparkling wines from areas other than Champagne. Crémant de Bourgogne Rosé and Crémant d'Alsace Rosé, both based on Pinot Noir, are very well priced, great for entertaining or gifting.

Italy produces light, crisp, and beautifully dry Pinot Noirs (called Pinot Nero here) that are dialed back, very light and soft-spoken, but which are delightful with delicate dishes. The best are found in the north, in Pinot Grigio areas Trentino-Alto Adige and Friuli-Venezia Giulia. There are excellent sparkling wines as well—Ferrari in Trento, Banfi Cuvée Aurora in Piedmont, and Bottega Liquid Metals are good names to seek out. Italy does serious Champagne-method sparkling wines in Lombardy's Franciacorta and Oltrepò Pavese regions, which often include Pinot Nero in the blend. These are in high demand in nearby Milan during Fashion Week.

Pinot Noir thrives in North America. Toronto restaurant goers love Cave Spring's standout French-style Pinot Noir from nearby and very cool climate Niagara Peninsula in Ontario. The grapes ripen a bit more on the West Coast in Oregon, nestled into hillside vineyards in the Willamette Valley near Portland, and even more along the California coast. Mendocino's Anderson Valley, Sonoma's Russian River Valley and Sonoma Coast, Sonoma and Napa's overlapping Carneros, Monterey's Santa Lucia Highlands, and Bien Nacido and Sta. Rita Hills in Santa Barbara are the state's top producing areas, all providing cooling influences from the Pacific Ocean that serve to moderate the plentiful sunshine. (Note that Sta. Rita is the legal name, after a lawsuit by Santa Rita in Chile.)

The dramatic, isolated isles of New Zealand are rich with idyllic to challenging vineyard areas. Pinot Noir loves a challenge and is a challenge, but it seems to calm down here. Oz Clarke says, "New Zealand has absolutely thrown the gauntlet down with Pinot Noir." New Zealand's only Master Sommelier, Cameron Douglas, says, "Pinot Noir is New Zealand's jewel. Sauvignon Blanc led the way, giving us the top ten hit we needed, and for over 25 years we have basked in its glory. Pinot Noir is getting us dangerously close to rock star status."

Central Otago near Queenstown on the South Island, nestled between the massive snow-capped Southern Alps to the west and the Pacific Ocean to the east, has proven that New Zealand will become known for more than just Sauvignon Blanc. North Canterbury near Christchurch, Sauvignon Blanc capital Marlborough and nearby Nelson and on the slightly warmer North Island, Martinborough near Wellington, and other areas are driving the Pinot train. We are in the beginning of something very special here. Stay tuned.

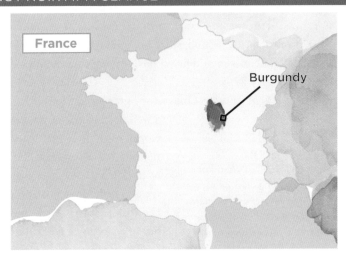

France: Burgundy, Champagne

Italy: Trentino-Alto Adige, Friuli-Venezia Giulia

Canada: Niagara

USA:

- Oregon: Willamette Valley
- California

New Zealand:

- South Island: Central Otago, North Canterbury, Marlborough, Nelson
- North Island: Martinborough

TASTE PROFILE AND STYLES

Pinot Noir is, as red wines go, feather-light in body, only getting richer as the grapes bask longer in the sun. Richer Pinot Noirs may spend time in oak, adding a gentle textural chewiness, and such flavors as vanilla, nutmeg, cinnamon, or cedar. The core aromas and flavors are red berries—tart cranberry, pomegranate, and raspberry, riper strawberry and cherry. Even though they are light and dry, their inviting, mouthwatering red berry notes give an impression of sweetness. From there, aside from any oak notes, you may find sun-dried tomato, red licorice, dried herbs, floral notes, earthy notes, and meaty notes.

Pinot Noir is called the most sensuous of wines because of its enticing, sometimes earthy perfume and soft, round, silky, but still lightly chewy texture. Even the richest, ripest Pinot Noirs should finish tart, leaving your mouth softly puckering, as if preparing for a kiss.

Pinot Noir is very light in color. One of the lightest red wines in the world is a well-aged Domaine de la Romanée-Conti, or DRC, the world's most famous red Burgundy. The praising of dark inky color as a sign of quality certainly does not apply here. If the Pinot Noir is dark and inky, it has likely been blended, diluted even, with another grape.

Pinot Noir–dominated sparkling wines are the richest in flavor and body. While sparkling wine typically is not fruity, the red berry notes often come out, giving these wines great food compatibility. Champagne from France and serious Italian and Californian sparkling wines are excellent examples. Italian Pinot Nero is generally light, unoaked, and tart.

Oregon's Willamette Valley Pinot Noirs look to Burgundy for stylistic inspiration but are riper and often more noticeably oaked, a style that is very popular in the USA.

In Northern California, Russian River Pinot Noirs often have a signature sarsaparilla, or root beer, note. In Santa Barbara, the flavors extend to clove-studded ham and bacon.

New Zealand Pinot Noirs are completely unexpected in their restraint, especially in light of the vivid, brash style of the region's much beloved Sauvignon Blancs.

New Zealand Pinot Noir

Here is a list of flavors I have compiled from my last two years of tasting New Zealand Pinot Noirs. I created lists like this when I was going through my Court of Master Sommelier exams. This deep dive was helpful in trying to sort out and recognize wines in the blind tasting exams.

- Red berry fruit—cranberry, pomegranate, raspberry, strawberry, cherry
- Sun-dried tomato, plum tomato, tomato paste
- Dried herbs—sage, marjoram, mint, fennel, bay leaf
- Spices—cumin, black pepper
- Floral—pink rose, red rose, violet
- Meaty—salami, pepperoni, wild game sausage, beef stew
- Earthy—wild mushroom, seared mushroom, sesame, terra-cotta

Old and New World Pinot Noir
Pick up a French Pinot Noir and one from the New World. Have a partner or friend pour them into two glasses and see whether you can tell which is which. What were the similarities? What were the differences? Was your mouth puckering to a kiss? Which did you prefer?

MUSICIAN

Alicia Keys possesses the quintessential voice of a woman: alluring, feminine, delicate, intoxicating, earthy, and haunting, while at the same time expressing a quiet, forceful undercurrent of power, like Pinot Noir.

DATING PROFILE

- I am pale and thin but my soul runs deep.
- My scent is intoxicating and memorable.
- I like to party, if I am in the mood.
- Go ahead, date someone more proper. You'll be thinking of me the whole time.
- I am earthy if not exactly down-to-earth.
- I don't know why people think I am a diva. My tastes are simple. I only like the best.

MATCHMAKING

Pinot Noir with mushrooms is one of nature's rare and exquisite gifts to the senses. Chicken, turkey, and quail play on the grape's earthiness well. Searing or char-ring fish, such as ahi or salmon, or meats plays nicely with the delicate fruit and tartness. Good Rosé Champagne—rich, layered, and struc-tured for food—pairs surprising well with lamb, as do still Pinot Noirs.

EVERY DAY WITH PINOT NOIR

RED BURGUNDY

Quail, duck confit, pasta with truffle butter

ROSÉ CHAMPAGNE

Lamb loin, fried chicken

ITALIAN PINOT NERO

Mushroom risotto

ITALIAN SPARKLING ROSÉ

Mushroom tart

AMERICAN PINOT NOIR

Salmon, BBQ chicken, mushroom quinoa—a great choice for Thanksgiving!

NEW ZEALAND PINOT NOIR

Chargrilled venison, lamb with star anise, cauliflower puree, Asian eggplant

CHEESE
Soft, creamy Brie
Ripe, fragrant Époisses

INSTA DINNER
Lean Cuisine—Beef Pot Roast
Marie Callender's—Roast Turkey Breast and Stuffing

UPSCALE CONVENIENCE
Homemade by Ayesha Curry—Portobello Mushroom Burgers with Herb Roasted Potatoes

SNACK
Ham and Brie sandwich

DINNER TONIGHT

CHICKEN AND MUSHROOM POTPIE

(OR JUST PIE, AS IT IS CALLED IN NEW ZEALAND)

Save time by just placing a top crust over a casserole dish or stoneware bowl or even individual ramekins, or buy a traditional dinner pie already prepared. Avoid spices. You want to be able to feel and taste the wine, after all.

Serve with the delicate, dry, tart, and fine Koha Pinot Noir, Marlborough $20; the fresh, delicate, supple, and shy Mt. Beautiful Pinot Noir, North Canterbury $25; or the full, soft, and both ripe and tart Landmark Overlook Pinot Noir, California $25.

SHOPPING

Like with anything in life that is so popular and in high demand, there are a lot of duds, especially at entry-level pricing. Finding a good Pinot Noir under $20 is virtually impossible. Don't get me wrong. There are many very popular brands in the midteens, but they are frankly not very drinkable. Do you remember the movie *Sideways*? This comedy was filmed in Santa Barbara and the signature red there is Pinot Noir. After the movie came out, people who had never tried it started asking for it and Pinot Noir went the way of Merlot—a lot of overpriced bad wine became available at every turn. This is why it is helpful to read reviews by experienced, credentialed wine experts. We taste it first. Read our reviews at planetgrapewine review.com, then make your decision. We put our palates on the line for you. Here are more than ten under $20, and lots more in the mid and upper tiers.

EVERYDAY VALUE/SHOPPING UNDER $20

Italy
Bottega Vinaia Pinot Nero, Trentino $18
> *Light, lithe, dry, and tart with notes of lemon zest, cranberry, raspberry, cherry, and pink rose*

Cavit Collection Pinot Nero, Provincia di Pavia $9
> *Dry, subtle, and silky with notes of lemon, cranberry, cherry, pink rose, and red licorice*

Sartori di Verona Pinot Noir, delle Venezie $13
> *Lean, fresh, light, and tart with notes of cherry, fennel seed, and lemon zest*

USA
Parducci Small Lot Pinot Noir, Mendocino $14
> *Silky and fresh with notes of strawberry, cherry, vanilla, and cedar*

Wild Horse Pinot Noir, Central Coast $18
> *Ripe and luscious with notes of strawberry, cherry, clove, and earthy coffee bean*

New Zealand
Babich Rosé of Pinot Noir, Marlborough $16
> *Dry, subtle, and crisp with notes of lime, strawberry, peach skin, and white rose*

Hunter's Pinot Noir Rosé, Marlborough $16
> *Dry, crisp, and vibrant with notes of lime, pink grapefruit, raspberry, peach, and ginger*

Matua Pinot Noir Rosé, Marlborough $14

Crisp and zingy with notes of raspberry, strawberry, chive, peach, and pineapple rind

Clos Henri Petit Clos Pinot Noir, Marlborough $16

Tart and lightly chewy with notes of strawberry, red rose, mushroom, plum tomato, and dark chocolate

Villa Maria Private Bin Pinot Noir, Marlborough $18

Tart, midweight, and vibrant with notes of cranberry, raspberry, red licorice, dill, crushed violet, and vanilla

Wither Hills Pinot Noir, Marlborough $14

Brisk and sweet-tart with notes of lemon, strawberry, watermelon, and crushed seashell (#beach)

VILLA MARIA NEW ZEALAND

Founded by Sir George Fistonich in 1961 in Auckland, Villa Maria has grown into one of New Zealand's most well-known and loved brands. The company has wineries in Marlborough on the South Island as well as in Auckland and Hawke's Bay on the North Island. I was very impressed to meet Helen Morrison, senior Marlborough winemaker, as we judged together over the course of three days, and enjoyed casual to more formal dinners at the 2017 Marlborough Wine Show. She is a breath of fresh air in our male-dominated wine world, and is the only woman on the company's winemaking team. Go get 'em, Helen!

IMPRESS YOUR GUESTS/SHOPPING $20-$50

France

Domaine Bertagna Les Dames Huguettes, Bourgogne Hautes-Côtes de Nuits $30

Soft, earthy, and tart with notes of raspberry, cherry, mushroom, dried leaves, leather, cinnamon, and cedar

Frédéric Esmonin, Bourgogne Hautes-Côtes de Nuits $26

Delicate, fresh, balanced, and tart with notes of raspberry, sage, white mushroom, and a touch of cedar

Joseph Faiveley, Bourgogne Pinot Noir $27

Light, dry, silky, and tart with notes of raspberry, cherry, rhubarb, summer squash, and cedar

Domaine Faiveley, Mercurey $30

Delicate, silky, fresh, and dry with notes of just-picked strawberries, moss, sage, and cedar

Allimant-Laugner, Crémant de Bourgogne Rosé $18

Fresh and fine with notes of raspberry, strawberry, whipped cream, and lemon zest

Italy

Banfi Cuvée Aurora Brut Rosé, Alta Langa $35

Elegant and subtle with notes of tangerine, strawberry, raspberry, almond, pretzel, and custard

Bottega Liquid Metals Rose Gold Vino Spumante Brut, Italy $35

Soft and sweet-tart with notes of pink grapefruit, strawberry, raspberry, mint, and chalk

Ferrari Brut Rosé, Trento $36

Very dry, fine, and chalky with notes of raspberry, strawberry, cantaloupe, banana nut bread, and gingerbread

Canada

Cave Spring Pinot Noir, Niagara Escarpment $20

Delicately silky, elegant, dry, and tart with notes of fresh raspberry, Bing cherry, pink rose, bay leaf, and nutmeg

USA

Ponzi Vineyards Pinot Noir Rosé, Willamette Valley $22

Soft, fruity, and tart with notes of cranberry, dried apricot, peach skin, watermelon, and green apple

Elizabeth Chambers Cellar Pinot Noir Falcon Glen, Willamette Valley $48

Inviting, silky, fresh, and dry with notes of raspberry, cherry, pomegranate, and pink rose

Montinore Estate Pinot Noir, Willamette Valley $20

Medium-bodied with cherry, maple, dark chocolate, and spice notes (Demeter Certified Organic)

Ponzi Vineyards Tavola Pinot Noir, Willamette Valley $27

Clean, fresh, vibrant, and dry with notes of sour cherry, plum, black currant, red licorice, cedar, and blackened ahi

Willamette Valley Vineyards Estate Pinot Noir, Willamette Valley $32

Richly fruity, dry, and elegant with notes of raspberry, cherry, cedar, mushroom, and sage

Artesa Pinot Noir Estate Reserve, Los Carneros, Napa Valley $45

Rich, round, and very ripe with notes of cherry, blackberry, violet, chocolate brownie, and caramel

Calera Pinot Noir, Central Coast $28

Full, silky, fresh, and dry with notes of raspberry, strawberry, mint, mushroom, and cedar

Cambria Benchbreak Pinot Noir, Santa Maria Valley $25

Bright, fresh, balanced, and tart with notes of cranberry, raspberry, violet, rose, cedar, and cinnamon

Dutton Goldfield Pinot Noir Dutton Ranch, Russian River Valley $44

Delicate in weight yet richly fruity with notes of raspberry, strawberry, and cherry along with notes of dried herbs, potpourri, and clove

Jackson Estate Pinot Noir, Anderson Valley $32

Silky and rich with notes of cranberry, raspberry jam, cherry Life Saver, rhubarb, cinnamon raisin bagel, clove-studded ham, black sesame seed, and red rose

Landmark Overlook Pinot Noir, California $25

Full, soft, and both ripe and tart with notes of raspberry, cherry, blueberry, boysenberry, black licorice, and tarragon

Lucia by Pisoni Vineyards Pinot Noir, Santa Lucia Highlands $45

Ripe and silky with fullness and finesse and notes of cranberry, raspberry, cherry, and earth

MacMurray Pinot Noir Estate Vineyards, Russian River Valley $23

Silky, layered, and fresh with notes of raspberry, strawberry, cherry, white rose, cedar, and vanilla

Melville Pinot Noir Estate, Sta. Rita Hills $36

Bright and vividly fruity with notes of raspberry, strawberry, cherry, vanilla bean, and warm hay

J Vineyards Brut Rosé, Russian River Valley $45

Strawberries dipped in fresh whipped cream and buttery croissants on a table set with fresh pink roses

Mumm Brut Rosé, Napa $24

Delicate, fine, and fresh with notes of strawberry wafer and lemon custard

New Zealand

Brancott Pinot Noir Terraces Southern Valleys, Marlborough $35

Light, tart, and dry with notes of cranberry, pomegranate, cherry, pink rose, mushroom, and thyme

Giesen Pinot Noir The Brothers, Marlborough $30

Ripe and fresh with notes of berry jam, plum, white rose, and clove

Koha Pinot Noir, Marlborough $20

Delicate, dry, tart, and fine with notes of cranberry, strawberry, cherry, tomato leaf, fennel seed, and rosemary

Nobilo Icon Pinot Noir, Marlborough $22

Ripe, sultry, and perfumed with notes of raspberry, cherry, pomegranate, red rose, red licorice, and cinnamon stick

Saint Clair Pinot Noir Awatere Valley, Marlborough $32

Expressive, beautifully silky, fresh, and delicate with notes of apricot, cranberry, strawberry, cherry cola, black pepper, sage, and nutmeg

te Pā Pinot Noir, Marlborough $24

Soft, subtle, feathery, and tart with notes of cranberry, pomegranate, cherry cola, bay leaf, and pink rose

Villa Maria Pinot Noir Taylors Pass, Marlborough $26

Elegant, dry, tart, and silky with notes of raspberry, cherry, pink rose, vanilla, and black licorice

Neudorf Pinot Noir Tom's Block, Nelson $26

Fresh, bright, lightly chewy, and dry with notes of black cherry, red licorice, brown mushroom, sage, espresso bean, and cedar

Greystone Pinot Noir Waipara Valley, North Canterbury $35

Subtle, tart, and feather light with notes of lemon peel, cranberry, raspberry, and earth

Mt. Beautiful Pinot Noir, North Canterbury $25

Fresh, delicate, supple, and shy with notes of strawberry, cherry, pink and yellow rose, moss, mushroom, and cedar, and a long raspberry rose finish

Mt. Difficulty Pinot Noir Bannockburn, Central Otago $45

Deeply flavorful, nicely balanced, and lightly chewy with notes of raspberry, cherry, and black pepper spice

Peregrine Pinot Noir, Central Otago $40

Soft, savory, and dry with notes of watermelon rind, cherry, red rose, thyme, cumin, and coriander

WORTH THE SPLURGE/SHOPPING $50 AND ABOVE

France

Domaine Antonin Guyon, Chambolle-Musigny $76

Light, fresh, gentle, and dry French Pinot Noir with notes of orange zest, raspberry, strawberry, dried rose petal, and mushroom

Domaine Henri Gouges, Nuits-St-Georges $57

Classy, fine, and delicate but with an underlying power, this silky French Pinot Noir has notes of raspberry, strawberry, black cherry, black tea, and prosciutto

Domaine Faiveley, Mercurey Clos des Myglands Premier Cru $53

Youthful, dry, lightly chewy, and lemony fresh with notes of pomegranate, strawberry, fennel seed, bay leaf, brown mushroom, and nutmeg

Domaine Vincent Girardin, Gevrey-Chambertin $55

Tart and elegant with notes of raspberry, cherry, earth, mushroom, tomato leaf, sumac, sandalwood, and exotic spice

Moët & Chandon Rosé Imperial Brut, Champagne $60

Easygoing, dry, and soft with notes of bright citrus, tart raspberry, spicy turmeric, and chalky minerality

USA

Foxen Pinot Noir La Encantada, Sta. Rita Hills $62

Ripe and beautifully balanced with notes of mandarin, watermelon, cranberry, cherry cobbler, root beer, and sandalwood

New Zealand

Giesen Pinot Noir Clayvin Southern Valleys, Marlborough $70

Organically farmed hillside fruit gives depth and intensity, but the expression is still fresh and delicate with notes of raspberry, cherry, mushroom, and tar

Nautilus Estate Pinot Noir Clay Hills, Marlborough $70

Youthful, chewy, dry, and rich with notes of blackberry, boysenberry, beef stew, fennel, and orange zest

Palliser Estate Pinot Noir The Great Ted, Martinborough $63

Youthful, rich, chewy, and fresh with notes of berry compote, rhubarb, violet, and cumin

Felton Road Pinot Noir Bannockburn, Central Otago $65

Delicate, layered, juicy, and fresh with notes of raspberry, cherry, white flowers, and lemon zest

Two Paddocks Pinot Noir The Fusilier, Central Otago $80

Youthful, dry, tart, and complex with notes of cherry, peppered salami, cumin, banana bread, mint, and violet

DINING OUT

Open the wine list to France, then Burgundy. As you now know, red Burgundy is French Pinot Noir. Since Old World sections are usually organized geographically, rather than varietally (by the grape), see whether you recognize any of the Côte de Nuits villages, or perhaps something from Mercurey. Burgundy will range in price from about $40 to $4,000 and up, so this is not a decision to take lightly.

It is practical to seek out either a producer you might be familiar with, such as Frédéric Esmonin, or a négociant, such as Faiveley or Louis Jadot. The difference between a producer and a négociant is land ownership. Most producers own their own estates, or vineyards. Négociants may have their own land holdings, but in general they purchase fruit from well-known vineyards and then bottle it with their own label, or brand. In the past, négociant wines were less than exciting, but these days they are producing reliable to spectacular wines. Just as with the producers, it is always good to try their entry-level wines first, then, if you like those, move up to something pricier from them.

Let's look at Faiveley, a well-known négociant. These are retail prices, so you can double or even triple them to get an idea of what they would be in a restaurant.

Faiveley
Bourgogne Rouge

$27

Faiveley
Mercurey

$30

Faiveley
Mercurey Premier Cru
Clos des Myglands

$53

The largest region, Bourgogne, is the source of the first wine. Then we move to Mercurey in southern Burgundy, and finally to an individual vineyard within Mercurey. You see that the smaller and more specialized the area the grapes come from, the pricier the wines get. With a good producer, the quality improves as well.

Now let's look at Frédéric Esmonin.

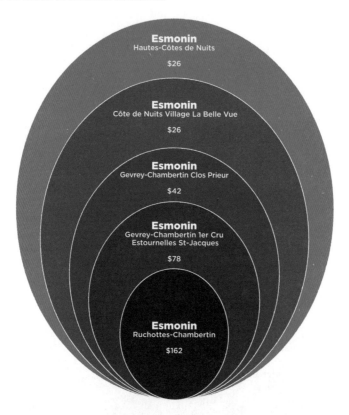

Look at the graphic to see how we are telescoping geography, starting with the regional Hautes-Côtes de Nuits area, and zooming in all the way to a tiny plot with 50-plus-year-old vines.

When selecting California and Oregon Pinot Noir from a restaurant wine list, it is helpful to look for familiar brands. If there is a sommelier on hand, ask for something similar in price and style to what you already know, so you can try something new. If you like what they recommend, go for it. If you feel you are being pressured into spending more money than you intended, ask the sommelier for a moment, and regroup.

Selecting from New Zealand is easy. For an area so highly successful with a white grape, the red producers feel the need to try very hard to match that. They are incredibly concerned with quality and trying to build a reputation for what is sure to become their signature red. In general, New Zealand Pinot Noirs skew lighter and tarter and leaner than any other New World region. However, the fruit is really ripe and approachable. In Central Otago, especially in earlier vintages, the wines achieved a richness and ripeness that paired well with toasty oak, but most producers have backed off of this, instead letting the wine speak of its origin, letting the wine express the uniqueness of its vineyard environment.

As with other regions, one thing that is helpful is to look for more rather than less geography in the name. If one of the wine labels reads "Catherine's Pinot Noir, New Zealand," and another reads "Catherine's Pinot Noir Single Vineyard Block, Bannockburn, Central Otago New Zealand," which do you think will be more interesting?

OPPOSITES ATTRACT

"You are the one with the class," my boyfriend always told me. I was 29. He was 45. I was living a bohemian life in Manhattan. He lived on an estate in upstate New York. I had traveled throughout greater Europe and North Africa on $5 a day, sleeping in youth hostels, or camping out on luggage racks on overnight train rides. His idea of roughing it was downgrading to a four-star hotel. I had been arrested for nude sunbathing in Cinque Terre, Italy. He had never skinny-dipped, so I took him to the nude beaches of French Saint Martin. I may have had some class, learned perhaps from books, movies, and observation of others in my travels, but he had a budget far greater than anything I had ever seen. Yet, with all that money, he still wanted to see the world through my eyes.

He was intrigued by my involvement with wine. He suggested that we travel together to visit some of my favorite wine destinations. We ended up a few months later in one of the most famous vineyards of the world, Domaine de la Romanée-Conti, in the Côte d'Or, in Burgundy, France.

I was awestruck by the simplicity of it. It was just a vineyard, like many others I had seen before. Sure, this was a prime site with more than two centuries of history. But there were rows of vines, with dirt in between them, and a modest little stone gate with the great name etched into it. That was it.

We drove right up to the gate, parked, and stepped freely into the vineyards. We were completely alone. As far as we knew, we were not being observed. I couldn't imagine that anyone could just waltz in like this, but there we were, and I was speechless.

I was so engrossed in my surroundings, bending down to observe the clusters of precious grapes, touching the vines, examining the shoots, digging my toes in the soil, that I didn't even notice what my dear friend was up to. I heard the sound of water, and I thought, "That's odd. I don't see any irrigation tubes, and there is no one around here." So I turned around, and, utterly horrified, watched as my soon to be ex-boyfriend finished taking a whiz right onto a vine! He said, "This year's harvest will be even better now."

That night, we ambled into a friendly looking Auberge St-Vincent in the town of Beaune, a central hub and a great base for exploring Burgundy. The restaurant was named after the patron saint of Burgundy. Even though our palates were fatigued—we had visited five properties that day—I was still feeling like a kid in a candy store. I couldn't wait to see what gems we might find on that wine list. But before I even had a chance to open it, my now for-sure-soon-to-be-ex-boyfriend said to the waiter, "Bring us a couple of Heinekens. We've had enough of your wine around here." The waiter's expression mirrored my own, though my skin was the shade of a fiery red beet.

A hush fell over the entire room. Even the non-French were looking down their noses at us, and thinking, "What an insult! What crass behavior! *Mon dieu!*" I wanted to crawl into a cave and never come out.

Was I upset? Yes. Was I humiliated? You bet. Hmm. I guess that is how my friend felt as he stared, standing in water up to his waist, unencumbered by swim trunks, at the shoreline of that nude beach in Saint Martin. I had egged him on to take off his shorts and go for a swim. I had promised to apply sunscreen anywhere on his body he so desired when he came back, knowing that I had a bottle of spray-on lotion in my bag. It was early, and only a few stragglers were on the beach. So he went for it. By now, however, several families with small children had arrived, and he was absolutely mortified. He begged and pleaded, as I stood, fully clad in my bathing suit, on the shore, taunting him. I wonder, now, looking back on that glorious day, how long he had been plotting his revenge.

BRANCH OUT

GAMAY

Gamay, which was banned from Burgundy in 1395, thrives in Beaujolais at the southernmost point in Burgundy where the soil changes from limestone and marl (great for Chardonnay and Pinot Noir) to schist. Gamay is more prone to produce wines that consistently deliver pleasure, in a style very close to those from the Côte d'Or—pretty berry fruit, tart lemony freshness, very little noticeable oak, and a silky texture, all very accessible and much more reliable than the crapshoot that is Burgundy.

Try one or both of these Beaujolais (Gamay) wines.

Chanrion, Côte de Brouilly Cru Beaujolais $16
   Fresh, light, and dry with notes of wild strawberry, pink rose, and lemon zest
Domaine Dupeuble, Beaujolais $16
   Light, fresh, tart, and clean with notes of cherry, blueberry, and blackberry

These are both imported by Kermit Lynch Wine Merchant, an importer and distributer based in Berkeley, California. As mentioned in the introduction, odds are if you like one, you will like the other. You will probably be happy with other wines in the selection as well. Shopping by importer is one way to up the odds of getting a wine you like.

Check Your Success Quiz

1. If red Burgundy is Pinot Noir, what grape makes white Burgundy?
2. Since New Zealand is considered a New World wine region, it is safe to say its Pinot Noirs are as rich, ripe, and lavishly oaked as many of those in California. Yes/No

---

ROSÉ

At a private beach club in Ramatuelle on the Saint-Tropez penin-sula, under the shade of pine, feet nestled into soft Provençal sand, I learned about wine in the best possible way. I observed a pack of playboys moving in on a bevy of beautiful women who were busy nibbling on seafood and sipping rosé. Nothing unusual here, or was there? Hmm. Wait a minute. The men were drinking pink, too. As it turns out, everyone, including the pale, plump, far too scantily clad Northern Europeans, was in on the game. It was just what you drank. Then, you took a nap.

What a great lesson that was, back in the Côte d'Azur. It made me realize that the French really didn't know so much more than us about wine. They simply drank what everyone else did, when everyone else did. It was summer, it was hot, and you drank rosé.

While coral was the color of most wines during Greek and Roman times, Provincia Romana, or today's Provence, is still considered the rosé center of the world. Early Bordeaux, or Clairet, was pink and so was early Californian wine. But it wasn't until a stuck fermentation that inspired the semisweet rosé of Zinfandel at Sutter Home did this pale beauty get its bad rap.

These days, pink wine is taken much more seriously, especially when pressed directly after skin contact. Other production methods include *saignée*—bleeding the tank—letting out juice that is already lightly colored, and blending white and red grapes, a method which is allowed and used in Champagne.

Rosé wines are still to fully sparkling, bone dry to decadently sweet, and produced all over the world. From light, tart French and Italian rosés to full-bodied, varietally expressive New World choices, it may be time to think about expanding pink wine options beyond the warm summer months. In particular, rosé sparkling wines pair surprisingly well with meaty main courses, such as lamb or duck breast.

These selections are recommended also within their respective grape chapters:

Still

Mouton Cadet Rosé, Bordeaux $11
  Light, dry, fresh, and mellow Merlot-based wine with notes of lemon zest, wild strawberry, and wintergreen
Attems Pinot Grigio Ramato (Rosé), Venezia Giulia $20
  Silky, light, and tart rosé with notes of lemon, raspberry, strawberry, and violet

Bertani Bertarose, Veneto $16

Subtle, delicate, mouthwatering, and dry with notes of strawberry, cantaloupe, pink rose, and sea spray

Mazzei Belguardo Rosé, Toscana $16

Light, dry, and fresh with notes of lemon sorbet, tangy strawberry yogurt, and nutmeg

Ponzi Vineyards Pinot Noir Rosé, Willamette Valley $22

Soft, fruity, and tart with notes of cranberry, dried apricot, peach skin, watermelon, and green apple

Ruby Vineyard Rosé of Pinot Gris, Willamette Valley $20

Dry and refreshing with notes of strawberry, rhubarb, and green tea

Gallo Family Vineyards White Zinfandel, California $4

Pleasantly sweet and juicy with notes of watermelon, strawberry, and lime Jell-O

Hess Collection Small Block Series Syrah Rosé, Napa Valley $22

Bone dry, racy, and bold with notes of raspberry, sour cherry, pomegranate, and white rose petal

Lake Sonoma Winery Rosé, Sonoma Valley $20

Refreshing, dry, and tart with notes of tangerine, strawberry, watermelon, oregano, and lavender

Peachy Canyon Rosé, Paso Robles $24

Full and juicy with notes of peach, strawberry, watermelon, and pink rose

Babich Rosé of Pinot Noir, Marlborough $16

Dry, subtle, and crisp with notes of lime, strawberry, peach skin, and white rose

Hunter's Pinot Noir Rosé, Marlborough $16

Dry, crisp, and vibrant with notes of lime, pink grapefruit, raspberry, peach, and ginger

Matua Pinot Noir Rosé, Marlborough $14

Crisp and zingy with notes of raspberry, strawberry, chive, peach, and pineapple rind

Sparkling

Allimant-Laugner, Crémant de Bourgogne Rosé $18

Fresh and fine with notes of raspberry, strawberry, whipped cream, and lemon zest

Moët & Chandon Rosé Imperial Brut, Champagne $60

Easygoing, dry, and soft with notes of bright citrus, tart raspberry, spicy turmeric, and chalky minerality

Banfi Cuvée Aurora Brut Rosé, Alta Langa $35

Elegant and subtle with notes of tangerine, strawberry, raspberry, almond, pretzel, and custard

Bottega Liquid Metals Rose Gold Vino Spumante Brut, Italy $35

Soft and sweet-tart with notes of pink grapefruit, strawberry, raspberry, mint, and chalk

Ferrari Brut Rosé, Trento $36
  Very dry, fine, and chalky with notes of raspberry, strawberry, cantaloupe, banana nut bread, and gingerbread
J Vineyards Brut Rosé, Russian River Valley $45
  Strawberries dipped in fresh whipped cream and buttery croissants on a table set with fresh pink roses
Mumm Brut Rosé, Napa $24
  Delicate, fine, and fresh with notes of strawberry wafer and lemon custard

BEACH WINE

Rosé is one of America's go-to beach wines. Summer in a glass. But summer goes so quickly. Why not extend the feeling with a little pink still or sparkling wine to keep the mood sunny?

Let me share a little story from my days as wine director/sommelier at a famous Bay Area restaurant. One day a new owner appeared, a French chef who had his own sommelier coming in a few months. I felt obligated to stay on, though it became more challenging by the day. One evening a group of his chef buddies came in and he was showing off by mixing up the ten-course tasting menu. Instead of finishing with the biggest, richest meat dish, which was paired with a big, bold red, he ended with bouillabaisse, the traditional Provençal fish stew. The classic pairing for this is the crisp white Cassis Blanc, but to end with a light white was something I just couldn't stomach, so I compromised and brought out Rosé de Provence. When Chef saw me pouring it, he came right up to my side and said very loudly, "What are you doing? We don't serve bitch wine here! Take it away."

At that moment the entire dining room came to a standstill, and I walked quickly away to find something else to offer them. That's when it hit me. He was saying "beach wine"—*beetch wine*, for the French.

6

SANGIOVESE

grape goddess says:
"San-gee-oh-vay-see." Repeat after me: "San-gee-oh-vay-see."

Sangiovese is not globally grown, with its best versions coming only from the Mediterranean center of Italy—Tuscany. It is not globally loved, either, however inoffensive it is even in its simplest form. But to say that I am head over heels in love with Sangiovese would be an understatement. Due in large part to its inherent zesty freshness and tartness, Sangiovese is about as far as one can get from being a cocktail wine. This light, tart, bitter red is going to make your mouth pucker, like Pinot Noir, as if preparing for a kiss, and water, anticipating another bite of food. No other red grape has the potential to give us a wine with so much complexity even at its lightest, and the ability to make food taste so good.

Because of its overwhelming popularity as Chianti, from Tuscany, Italy, there is unfortunately a lot of mediocre Sangiovese in the market. In the United States, it is sold in thousands of Italian chain and independent restaurants, as well as in every grocery store and wine shop. It is considered a prerequisite. Cabernet. Check. Chardonnay. Check. Chianti. Check. This is the wine that used to come in the basket-weave-covered flask, a *fiasco*—literally. Some still do. Stay far away from those unless you need a candle holder or lamp base. It is likely you've already been underwhelmed with this light, pale, distinctly unfruity red. Which is why I am including this lean, mean machine of a grape, so you can discover how to choose a great Sangiovese, and then discover its true potential at the table, where it shines as bright as the Tuscan sun.

HISTORY

As early as 1590, Italian author Giovanni Vittorio Soderini noted Sangiogheto or Sangioveto as a reliable producer in his *La Coltivazione delle Viti* (*The Growing of Grapes*). St. John, or San Giovanni, may have been an early inspiration for its name, but the most famous story is that Sangiovese is the blood of Jove, the Roman god Jupiter. It is likely that Sangiovese was growing wild in Tuscany and the surrounding regions during Etruscan times.

GEOGRAPHY

Sangiovese is grown all over Italy, blended with the local grapes or bottled on its own, producing a cheap and cheerful light dry red. Although pleasant to sip while there, these are not so interesting at home. Sangiovese di Romagna from Emilia-Romagna, Rosso Piceno in the Marches, and Umbria's Montefalco Rosso are often in this lighter, straightforward style.

The best Sangiovese in the world comes from Tuscany. Sangiovese thrives in this quintessential Mediterranean climate. The lightest, simplest of these come from the places called Chianti, a large swatch of central Tuscany; and Morellino di Scansano, from the southwest coast. Sangiovese grown anywhere in Tuscany can be blended and called Sangiovese di Toscana, similar to a wine labeled "California," rather than "Sonoma, California." As we telescope down to the smaller areas, Sangiovese sings like diva Maria Callas as Chianti Classico, Brunello di Montalcino, and Vino Nobile di Montepulciano. For now, let's shorten these to CC, BdM, and VNdM, respectively.

In Chianti Classico, nestled between the cities of Florence and Siena, days are warm and nights are cool. Montalcino to the south of Siena is warmer still, giving richer, lightly fruitier wines that can handle oak treatment. In fact the name Brunello (in BdM), translates to "little brown one," as if Sangiovese went there to get a tan.

Richer, oakier versions of CC, BdM, and VNdM wines, with the term Riserva on the label, are the most serious, whereas Rosso di Montalcino and Rosso di Montepulciano are simpler, lighter, and less pricey—the training-wheel versions. Gran Selezione is the summit of the Chianti Classico appellation. It requires the use of estate-grown fruit plus 30 months' aging.

The producer Antinori's Tignanello, in the category known as Super Tuscan, is right up there in the winner's circle as well. Tignanello is Sangiovese nicely enriched with a little Cabernet Sauvignon for color, depth, and a little dark fruit.

> **When in Rome**
>
> Almonds may prevent intoxication. The Roman custom of eating salted almonds throughout the meal goes back to the days of Dracus, the father of Emperor Tiberius, who claimed to have remained sober despite consuming copious quantities of wine by constantly eating almonds. Meditrina, the Roman goddess of wine, probably gave him the idea.
>
> Almonds are laden with vitamin E, protein, fiber, magnesium, iron, calcium, and phosphorous, and these crunchy little nuggets are antioxidants to boot.

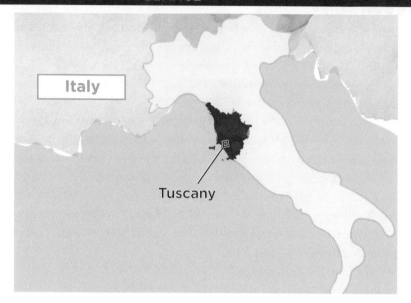

Italy:

- Tuscany
    - Chianti: Chianti Classico (CC), Chianti Classico Riserva (CCR), Chianti Classico Riserva Gran Selezione (CCR+)
    - Montalcino: Rosso di Montalcino, Brunello di Montalcino (BdM), Brunello di Montalcino Riserva
    - Montepulciano: Rosso di Montepulciano, Vino Nobile di Montepulciano (VNdM), Vino Nobile di Montepulciano Riserva
    - Carmignano
    - Morellino di Scansano
    - Super Tuscan—Tignanello
- Umbria (Montefalco Rosso)
- Marches (Rosso Piceno)
- Emilia-Romagna (Sangiovese di Romagna)

USA: California

This blend is done as well in Carmignano, but more than 10 to 20 percent of rich Cabernet added to light Sangiovese will fully dominate its character.

In the USA, Sangiovese was on the rise as more Italian chain and individual restaurants opened up in the 1980s. Napa Valley's Tra Vigne restaurant asked local vintners to produce a Sangiovese so it could serve local wines. But Sangiovese is not so easy to grow as the ubiquitous Cabernet Sauvignon or Chardonnay, and even producers such as Antinori, who planted the grape at their Antica Napa Valley winery, have switched to Cabernet Sauvignon. The market also didn't respond enthusiastically. California Sangiovese has never has become as popular as Merlot, Cabernet Sauvignon, or the latest darling, Pinot Noir.

TASTE PROFILE AND STYLES

Have you ever traveled around Europe by train? If so, you may have noticed that from north to south the climate, and the culture, changes dramatically. The wine styles follow this pattern as well, with cooler northern wines and locals more reserved, whereas warmer-climate wines and people are more open, relaxed, and friendly. At the train station in Paris, a person may get an air kiss or two on the cheeks. In southern France, an actual kiss. In Milan, four kisses, two on each cheek, and a warm hug, and by the time you reach Rome, it is very nearly an orgy. Tuscany sits firmly on the friendly side and its wines make you want to kiss. That is, because they are chewy, tart, bone dry, and bitter!

Like Pinot Noir, the wines are light in color and share both cherry and mushroom as characteristics. The cherry in Sangiovese is closer to Morello than Bing, and is always ripe. There may be notes of strawberry, plum, sun-dried tomato, dried herbs, lavender, licorice, and leather. When oaked, there may be a little cedar or vanilla and a gentle chewiness or grip. Sangiovese wines are zesty, having both a gently gripping chewiness from the grape skins and oak, if used, combined with vivid natural acidity. Still, they have a great deal of finesse, elegance, and intrigue.

New World Sangioveses, like those from California, are often styled with noticeable to overwhelming oak characters, and have both higher alcohol and much lower acidity, as the grapes are fully ripe to overripe. In such areas as Napa Valley, Sonoma, the Central Coast, and in the Sierra Foothills near Lake Tahoe, the grape ripens well but gets lost under traumatic oak treatment. The exceptions to the rule are noted in our Shopping section.

MUSICIAN

Light and lean, soft-spoken, and romantic, Usher seduces us slowly and quietly with his words. He makes us wanna leave the one we're with. Then, he makes us wait for it, wait for it.

DATING PROFILE

- I'm Italian.
- I am sensitive and sometimes moody.
- I am bitter, in a sophisticated way.
- I have been called arrogant once or twice, but at heart am humble and down-to-earth.
- I really need my partner, food, to show off my assets. We are a package deal.

SENSE EXERCISE

Licorice

A typical Italian farmer's market has a booth or two selling dozens of types of black or red licorice. It tastes very strong, and a little salty compared to American licorice candy—think Twizzlers or Red Vines. Italian licorice is hard to come by here, but excellent versions from Australia are available in many specialty groceries. Trader Joe's carries the excellent Panda brand from Switzerland. Obtain a bag of red licorice and one of black. Open your Sense notebook. Find a quiet, well-lit, odor-free nook. Jot down a few descriptors for both. Do this again a few days later. Finally, do this a third time. Now, go back with a highlighter and note any words that keep coming up—words you have repeated again and again. Excellent. You have now isolated a few licorice descriptors. These will stick with you.

Now open a Sangiovese and jot down a few descriptors. And don't be surprised if you've plugged in one or two from the licorice exercise. This is how you expand your descriptor toolbox. *Eccellente! Ottimo lavoro!* Good job!

Ten Grapes to Know

SUPER TUSCANS

Sassicaia is a wine known and loved the world over. From a beautiful coastal hamlet in Tuscany, this Super Tuscan blend is, hands down, Italy's most famous wine. It is also the world's second-most-counterfeited wine after Château Pétrus.

So, what is behind this success story? In 1948, the Marchese Mario Incisa della Rocchetta began a revolution in Tuscan winemaking, and not in the traditional wine region of Tuscany, Chianti Classico, but at a large farm in the village of Bolgheri, located close to Tuscany's Mediterranean coastline in the southwestern part of the province.

It was here, at Tenuta San Guido, that Mario decided to plant Cabernet Sauvignon and Cabernet Franc vine cuttings that he had received from his buddy at Château Lafite-Rothschild in Bordeaux. The marchese made a non-traditional wine from these non-traditional grapes planted on a nontraditional site. The wine, Sassicaia, which Mario made for his family and friends, was aged in nontraditional French *barriques*—small French oak barrels—not the classic old Slavonian oak casks preferred by Tuscan producers

Mario's brother-in-law, Marchese Niccolò Antinori and his son, Piero, realized the commercial potential of Sassicaia. Working with Mario's son, (also named Niccolò), Antinori winemaker Giacomo Tachis, and Bordeaux-based enologist Émile Peynaud, the Antinori family brought Sassicaia to market in 1968. It was wildly successful, and the "Super Tuscan" era had begun. Piero then went on to produce Tignanello, a Super Tuscan based on his beloved Sangiovese.

Dottore Sebastiano Rosa, stepson of Niccolò Incisa della Rocchetta, was born in Rome in 1966, but by 1968 was living in Bolgheri. As a young adult, Dr. Rosa came to California to study at UC Davis, graduating in 1990. While in California, he worked at Jordan Winery and Stag's Leap Wine Cellars. In 1991, he spent a year at Château Lafite-Rothschild, and for the next decade he worked with Giacomo Tachis, the father of the renaissance of Italian wine, as general manager at Tenuta di Argiano in Montalcino at the invitation of owner Contessa Noemi Marone Cinzano. Today both Cinzano and Dr. Rosa's brother, Piero Incisa della Rocchetta, operate neighboring wineries in Patagonia, Argentina—Bodega Noemía and Bodega Chacra.

Although Dr. Rosa lives in Bolgheri with his wife, Elena, and stepson Edoardo, he has returned frequently to California to consult with Brooks Painter and Peter Velleno in making the delicious Tuscan-style wines for Castello di Amorosa. Castello di Amorosa is a 121,000-square-foot thirteenth-century medieval Tuscan-style castle and winery built by Dario Sattui in Napa Valley.

MATCHMAKING

Sangiovese has it in spades, the structural component that not only brings food into bright focus, but that serves to cleanse and refresh the palate—natural acidity. Italian Sangiovese is the only wine on earth that can literally stand up to a lemon wedge. Go ahead, squeeze or bite into a piece of lemon, then take a sip of Chianti. The wine is like, "Really, is that your best shot?" Now, try garlic, or olives, or even anchovies. Most of these food elements would make a red wine taste awful, but not Sangiovese. High-acid Sangiovese has a particular affinity for tomatoes, mushrooms, and herbs, and provides refreshment and balance to rich dishes. It is understated and elegant enough to showcase even the trendy "tweezer" food of the day.

EVERY DAY WITH SANGIOVESE

Breaded eggplant cutlets

Chicken liver pâté on country bread

Fried porcini mushrooms

Pan-roasted white fish with bacon

Risotto

Skirt steak with mushrooms

Veal saltimbocca

CHEESE

Pecorino

INSTA DINNER

Amy's Bowls—Cheese Ravioli

Lean Cuisine—Comfort Steak Portabella

UPSCALE CONVENIENCE

Plated—Skillet Grandma (Pizza) Pie with Parmesan-Kale Salad

WEEKENDS IN TUSCANY

Working as a nanny and English tutor, I lived nearly expense-free in Florence for eight months. At the beginning of fall, the family drove out to the countryside, the hills of Chianti, and picked up a *damigiana* (demijohn) of wine, along with a slightly smaller vat of just-harvested olive oil. Life from that point on got even better.

SNACK

Parmigiano-Reggiano drizzled with balsamic vinegar, prosciutto-wrapped breadsticks

---

DINNER TONIGHT

Here is a simple two-course dinner. Gather the components ahead of time and save any leftover wine for the weekend.

CROSTINI WITH KALE

Top grilled or toasted bread with kale sautéed in olive oil. Delicious with the crisp, refreshing Lake Sonoma Winery Rosé of Sangiovese, Sonoma Valley $20

GRILLED ITALIAN SAUSAGES/LENTIL SALAD

Grill or sauté the sausages and toss warm lentils into your favorite salad topped with olive oil and balsamic vinegar. Serve with the Rocca delle Macìe, Chianti Classico $16.

TUSCANY, BIRTHPLACE OF PUCCINI

Tuscany . . . this is the Italy of our dreams—the magical region we have read about, seen in paintings, and fantasized about. We can visualize it in our mind's eye: the olive groves, cypress trees, farms and vineyards, the medieval villages, walled hilltop towns, and Renaissance cities.

It is the land of Florence, Siena, Lucca, and the Chianti countryside, of the Uffizi and the Leaning Tower of Pisa and the countless duomos. It is the home of Dante, Galileo, Machiavelli, Leonardo da Vinci, Michelangelo, Puccini, and yes, even Gucci and Ferragamo.

And then there are the wines and the food. What would life be without Chianti Classico, Brunello, Vin Santo, or the Super Tuscans? Or crostini, biscotti, pecorino, Chianina beef, pappardelle, porcini, and panforte? Not to mention the fresh herbs, Tuscan olives, and extra-virgin olive oil.

The great noble families of Florence, such as de Medici, Ricasoli, Frescobaldi, Antinori, and Della Gherardesca, have tended the most wonderful farms in Chianti for centuries. From these farms and country vineyard estates was born a lifestyle of elegance and warm hospitality. It is an elegant society, but what is on the table is called peasant food. Locals are called *mangiafagioli*—bean eaters.

Most would agree that Emilia-Romagna is the culinary capital of Italy. I say Tuscany. When I returned from a four-day trip, there was nothing I wanted to eat at home. Bread, pecorino or Parmigiano cheese, pasta, olive oil, coffee, wine, beef, vegetables—you name it, so I lived on cabbage for about a week until I got over it (this was also an effective way to drop the extra pounds of which three were in focaccia alone).

SHOPPING

EVERYDAY VALUE/SHOPPING UNDER $20

Italy

Mazzei Belguardo Rosé, Toscana $16

Light, dry, and fresh with notes of lemon sorbet, tangy strawberry yogurt, and nutmeg

Caparzo Sangiovese, Toscana $15

Zesty, bright, lightly chewy, and fresh with notes of Bing cherry, fennel sausage, and seared mushroom

Folonari, Chianti $9

Light, tart, and dry with notes of strawberry, cherry, white mushroom, and pink rose

Rocca delle Macìe, Chianti Classico $16

Fresh, lean, lightly chewy, and tart with notes of cherry, brush, herbs, leather, and venison chop

Avignonesi, Rosso di Montepulciano $19

Light, tart, dry, and brisk with notes of Bing cherry, sage, cedar, lemon verbena, and fennel sausage

La Ciarliana, Rosso di Montepulciano $16

Easygoing, supple, and fruity with notes of Morello cherry, heirloom tomato, and tobacco

IMPRESS YOUR GUESTS/SHOPPING $20–$50

Italy

Borgo Scopeto, Chianti Classico $21

Dry, savory, and zesty with notes of cherry, mushroom, oregano, and leather

Castello di Gabbiano, Chianti Classico Riserva $25

Dry, tart, midweight, and nearly crunchy with notes of sour cherry, raspberry, nutmeg, leather, fennel, and green olive

Castello di Volpaia, Chianti Classico Riserva $30

Mellow and creamy, then brisk, dry, and lightly chewy with notes of sour plum, sundried tomato, oregano, Fernet-Branca, and pink rose

Fattoria di Fèlsina Rancia, Chianti Classico Riserva $40

Zesty and chewy with notes of raspberry, sour cherry, red licorice, truffle, potting soil, dried herbs, and osso buco

Melini La Selvanella, Chianti Classico Riserva $28

Zesty, tart, earthy, and dry with notes of cherry, mushroom, leather, and cinnamon

Pèppoli, Chianti Classico $28

Lively, fresh, dry, and tart with notes of cherry, stewed tomato, brown mushroom, bay leaf, and nutmeg

Querciabella, Chianti Classico $32

Balanced, lively, zesty, and lightly oaky with notes of cherry, stewed tomato, verbena, moss, carob, and cedar (biodynamic)

Ruffino Riserva Ducale Oro, Chianti Classico Gran Selezione $38

Elegant, refined, and silky with notes of sun-dried tomato, strawberry, dark cherry, stewed meats, prosciutto, mushroom, and licorice

Villa Antinori, Chianti Classico Riserva $35

Fresh, delicate, gently chewy, and dry with notes of cherry, leather, sage, brown mushroom, cumin, and lemon zest

Castello Banfi, Rosso di Montalcino $25

Tart, bright, and zesty with notes of cranberry, sour cherry, pomegranate, sun-dried tomato, dark chocolate, sautéed mushroom, and leather

Col d'Orcia, Rosso di Montalcino $25

Fresh, dry, tart, and chewy Sangiovese with notes of cherry, rose water, mushroom, sage, and black licorice

Avignonesi, Vino Nobile di Montepulciano $20

Silky, smooth, light, and supple with notes of Dr Pepper, red licorice, fennel, salumi, iron, tomato paste and cedar. Gently chewy and lemony fresh finish

Carpineto, Vino Nobile di Montepulciano Riserva $26

Chewy and lively with notes of cherry, chestnut, bacon, pepper salami, and earthy cheese

La Ciarliana, Vino Nobile di Montepulciano $26

Bordeaux-like in structure, this firm, fresh Sangiovese-based blend (95%) has notes of cherry, fruitcake, mint, red rose, beef stew, and musk

Trerose Santa Caterina, Vino Nobile di Montepulciano $35

Deliciously zippy, grippy, and fresh with notes of Bing cherry, black raisin, root beer, chestnut, sun-dried tomato, Italian herbs, porcini, and seared meat

USA

Lake Sonoma Winery Rosé of Sangiovese, Sonoma Valley $20

Refreshing, dry, and tart with notes of tangerine, strawberry, watermelon, oregano, and lavender

Chanticleer Sangiovese, Napa Valley $48

Lively, lightly chewy, fresh, and dry with notes of raspberry, cherry, bay leaf, mushroom, brisket, pink rose, chocolate truffle, and vanilla

Eberle Sangiovese, Paso Robles $34

Rich and lightly chewy with notes of cherry cola, plum, fig, red licorice, vanilla, and cocoa

Ferrari-Carano Siena Red, Sonoma $23

Full, supple, and fresh with notes of red cherry, pink rose, orange peel, and cedar

WORTH THE SPLURGE/SHOPPING $50 AND ABOVE

Italy

Badia a Passignano, Chianti Classico Riserva Gran Selezione $60

Fine, elegant, supple, and fresh with notes of cherry, black licorice, leather, fennel, coriander, and mushroom marinara

Castello d'Albola Il Solatio, Chianti Classico Gran Selezione $60

Balanced, expressive, fresh, and elegant with notes of cherry, black licorice, tobacco, cedar, maple, mushroom, and moss

Castello di Ama San Lorenzo, Chianti Classico Gran Selezione $52

Velvety, juicy, and dry with notes of cherry, earth, fennel seed, red rose, and espresso

Castello Banfi, Brunello di Montalcino $90

Youthfully gripping, tart, fresh, and dry with notes of cherry cola, red licorice, pink rose, beef stew, nutmeg, cinnamon, and vanilla

Col d'Orcia, Brunello di Montalcino $55

Full, robust, fresh, and lively with notes of strawberry, cherry, white rose, mushroom, dried thyme, vanilla, coffee bean, and cigar box

Il Poggione, Brunello di Montalcino $85

Rich and sweetly oaky with notes of sun-dried tomato, tomato paste, black and Bing cherry, salami, braised meats, earth, and leather; lush fruit mixes with chewy tannins

Val di Suga, Brunello di Montalcino $70

Rich and chewy with notes of sour cherry, sun-dried tomato, red licorice, button mushroom, new leather, cigar box, and moss

Valdicava, Rosso di Montalcino $50

Gently chewy with vibrant natural acidity and notes of cherry, red licorice, red rose, porcini, moss, sage, cumin, and singed meat

TIGNANELLO AND SOLAIA DINNER AT PÉPPOLI

Pebble Beach, California

With the promise of a Sunday morning tee time, Piero Antinori and wine-maker Renzo Cotarella jetted in to Pebble Beach Resorts in California several years ago to host a dinner showcasing their renowned Super Tuscans, the Cabernet-based Solaia and the Sangiovese-based Tignanello. Guests assembled at Pèppoli, a joint venture between the Antinori family and the Inn at Spanish Bay and named after the family's Pèppoli Estate in Tuscany. Pebble Beach Resorts cellarmaster Joseph Nase, previously of New York City's Lespinasse, called in his chips to assemble an awe-inspiring collection of wines dating back to 1983, including ultra-rare magnums of Secentenario, a classic Tignanello blend of 80 percent Sangiovese, 15 percent Cabernet Sauvignon, and 5 percent Cabernet Franc bottled in honor of Antinori's 600th anniversary (1385–1985).

Pèppoli chef Stephen Blackwell's menu paired seamlessly with the wines. His mastery of and passion for Tuscan wine and food pairing was obvious. At the last minute he added foie gras butter to the prawns based on a dream he had had the night before, "to help the dish stand up to the young wines." As guest sommelier I partnered with Joseph to open, decant, pretaste, and pour each flight of wines. Although we were intensely focused on clockwork wine service, the perfume of these wines, especially of the 1983 and 1986 Tignanello and of the Secentenario, stopped us in our tracks. The Solaias showed their cool, self-assured power, and deep, dark, brooding fruit. Both 1997s showed that rich, intense, ripe fruit character of their stellar vintage so appealing to crossover or neophyte consumers, while retaining the class and elegance favored by traditionalists.

For me, Tignanello is to Solaia as Burgundy is to Bordeaux. Tignanello's earthiness and its lithe, pure core of well-bred cherry fruit seduces on first encounter. Its bite and grip solidifies its reputation as a saucy little number, whereas drinking Solaia is like meeting with one's stockbroker on a good day. The atmosphere is strict but the impact of good news sends shivers of delight up and down one's spine just the same.

DINING OUT

Aside from Super Tuscan blends, Brunellos are the priciest of Tuscan wines. There is a way to circumvent the process a bit, though. Search for the training-wheels versions, or baby Brunellos—those from younger vines with less oak aging. These are called Rosso di Montalcino. They are lighter, more accessible earlier on, and far less chewy and drying. If your group is large enough, order one bottle each of the Banfi or Col d'Orcia Rosso di Montalcino and their Brunello. Start with the Rosso, then build up to the Brunello, and you will clearly be able to note their differences.

One of the best deals in Italian Sangiovese is Vino Nobile di Montepulciano. In the shadow of hefty, beefier Brunello di Montalcino and lighter, softer Chianti Classico Riservas, it never has gotten the acclaim it truly deserves. Rosso di Montepulciano is a great way to begin to experience wines of this area.

Another selection to look for is Chianti Classico Riserva with the addition on the label of "Gran Selezione," which indicates the fruit must be estate grown and that the wine will be held for aging at the winery for a minimum of 30 months before release.

LADIES WHO LUNCH

I had a nearly religious moment outside the Ferragamo shop in Florence. Walking Fifth Avenue as a young woman, I observed the uniform of Ladies Who Lunch: Chanel suit, Hermès bag, often with matching miniature dog, thick pearls, short coiffed hair, and Ferragamo patent leather Vara pump with the signature bow.

What I expected to see was a collection of polished, conservative block-heeled shoes and those little matching bags with the bows on them, like what is sold in America. But when I saw the outfit in the window—a stunning, swirling, feminine top, skirt, heels, and bag, I froze. I remember feeling goose bumps. This was design and craftsmanship at its finest. It was downright breathtaking. Way beyond my means at the time, I priced it at Duty Free on the way home. It would have only been around $3,000 there, but I had neither the cash nor a credit card at the time, so it still didn't make the cut. I will never forget it.

BRANCH OUT

NERO D'AVOLA

Like Sangiovese, Nero d'Avola is light and zesty, easy to pair with food. It is from Sicily, so there is just a touch more fruit and weight. Donnafugata's is one of my faves.

Donnafugata Sherazade Nero d'Avola, Sicilia $20

> *Light, dry, crisp, and expressive red with notes of strawberry, sour cherry, Nutella, brown mushroom, sea spray, and white flowers*

Check Your Success Quiz

1. Is Chianti Classico a good choice for wine to be served at a cocktail party? Yes/No
2. Brunello, or Sangiovese from Montalcino, means "little brown one" due to the warmer climate there, giving the grape a "suntan." True/False

---

7

SYRAH/SHIRAZ

Shiraz, the name widely used in Australia, and Syrah, that used in France and elsewhere, are the same grape. The Persian city of Shiraz is said to be its origin, and when it landed in France, they changed the name to Syrah.

For a grape that delivers so much pleasure, whether simple to complex, light and juicy to structured and rich, its popularity is very recent. In France, Syrah claims the Rhône Valley as its rightful home, blending with Grenache and Mourvèdre in the south for easy-to-enjoy Côtes du Rhône wines, and standing on its own on steep, terraced vineyards overlooking the river in the north. Well-situated hillsides Côte-Rôtie and Hermitage are the northern Rhône jewels and are considered the world's benchmark for Syrah.

Yet demand for these gems up until the 1980s was so low, while the market for the other classic French wines was hot, that many farmers simply sold their fruit to négociants. It wasn't until famous American wine critic Robert Parker "discovered" the great French Syrahs that they began to earn a reputation among collectors and sommeliers, though always in the shadow of the great red Bordeaux and Burgundy wines, at much lower prices, and far easier to acquire. Keep in mind, too, that with culinary capital Lyon and all of its thirsty restaurant patrons to the north, it is no surprise even the simplest wines are easy to sell. Why would producers need to make better wine?

HISTORY

Syrah, the offspring of Mondeuse Blanche and Dureza, is along with Chardonnay and Pinot Noir one of the world's oldest wine grapes. It is possible the grape we call Syrah was cultivated from wild vines in Roman Gaul.

An oft-told story begins in Shiraz, a city in the country known today as Iran. By one account, the knight Gaspard de Sterimberg brought cuttings of the plant from Shiraz to France's northern Rhône on his return from the Crusades in the thirteenth century. He lived like a hermit on a hill that was known as early as the sixteenth century as Hermitage.

With so many difficult vintages in Bordeaux, the area to the northwest known for blends based on Cabernet Sauvignon and Merlot, producers began adding small amounts of northern Rhône Syrah to round them out in body and to give a ripe, pleasant, plummy fruit character. This process, known as *hermitagé*, took place until the early 1900s.

Father of Australian viticulture James Busby brought the grape known as Scyras from the Rhône to Sydney, Australia, in 1832 to see whether it could withstand the hot climate there. It took hold quickly there and throughout the cooler growing areas, where it became known as Shiraz.

GEOGRAPHY

With one small if firm footprint in the Old World, France's Rhône Valley, and one supersize success story in the new, Australia, Syrah/Shiraz is here to stay. On the steep hillside vineyards of the northern Rhône, powerful Hermitage and more delicate, perfumed Côte-Rôtie are the king and queen of Syrah. Neighboring vineyard areas on the flats—Crozes-Hermitage, Saint-Joseph, and Cornas—produce sturdier and less complex versions. Without steep terraces along the river, the vines get less sun. Sun shines on the river, then reflects on the vines, giving them a double dose of sunshine. Ever heard of rotisserie chicken? Well, Côte-Rôtie literally translates to "roasted slope."

As with other grape growing areas, there is a spread of the popular grape into surrounding regions. These are known as satellite regions. The Collines Rhodaniennes, a large area surrounding the Rhône, produces lighter, fruitier, softer, and simpler Syrahs that are very wallet-friendly.

Syrah is also in use by winemakers in Tuscany, who bottle it alone or blend it in to plump up their lighter, more lithe Sangiovese wines.

Washington and California in the USA are successful areas for Syrah, with cooler sites along the California coast often producing the more restrained French styles. Chile and Argentina produce ripe, reliable, and well-oaked styles of Syrah.

South Africa's Coastal Region is a place to look for well-priced, everyday drinking Shiraz. If a producer there is modeling after the French style, it will label its wine as Syrah.

In Australia, where the grape is called Shiraz, South Australia standouts include Clare Valley, Eden Valley, McLaren Vale, and Barossa Valley. Hunter Valley in New South Wales produces distinctive Shiraz as well. Aussies have had to find areas where the grape can ripen, but not bake, in which case it would lose its trademark perfume. Like the Aussies themselves, these wines are friendly, outgoing, and in your face. No wallflowers here.

Hawke's Bay in New Zealand's warmer, sunnier North Island is home to that country's best Syrah, which like its Sauvignon Blanc is exquisitely ripe and brimming with fruit and fun. There are Old World styles as well, but with Aussie Shiraz so close, that is the model they tend to follow.

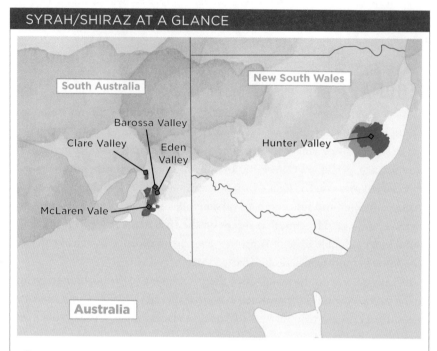

SYRAH/SHIRAZ AT A GLANCE

France:
- Northern Rhône Valley: Côte-Rôtie, Hermitage, Crozes-Hermitage, Saint-Joseph, Cornas
- Collines Rhodaniennes

Italy: Tuscany

USA: Washington, California

Chile

Argentina

South Africa: Coastal Region

Australia:
- South Australia: Clare Valley, Eden Valley, McLaren Vale, Barossa Valley
- New South Wales: Hunter Valley

New Zealand: North Island: Hawke's Bay

TASTE PROFILE AND STYLES

Sultry Syrah is deeply colored, often with a hot pink or magenta undertone. When less ripe, notes of black peppercorn bubble up along with floral perfume, as they often do in cooler vintages from France. Where the climate is warm, the grape ripens quickly and loses the pepper and perfume, instead showcasing jammy ripe fruit, which is then paired with sweet toasty oak.

The Rhône Valley's Côte-Rôtie and Hermitage, the world's finest examples of Syrah, are deeply colored, powerful, flavored with dark berry fruit, earth, smoke, bacon, lilacs, white and pink peppercorns, and herbes de Provence and have a long aging potential. They are medium-bodied and dry, as are less expensive appellations Saint-Joseph, Crozes-Hermitage, and Cornas, whose wines sometimes take on a rubbery or burnt tire character. In Italy, Syrah is grown in Tuscany, where it finds its way into many Super Tuscan and Chianti wines.

Washington (Columbia Valley) and California (Mendocino, Napa, Sonoma, Lodi, Monterey, Paso Robles, and Santa Barbara) are all producing Syrah in a wide variety of styles in the USA. In the warmer regions, the grape quickly loses finesse and perfume. In Washington's Columbia Valley, where they are often aged in American oak, the wines have a distinctive blueberry/mocha/roasted coffee bean flavor and are quite rich and dense. Syrahs from Mendoza, Argentina, are richly fruity and often oaked, yet balanced with fresh natural acidity. Chilean Syrahs shine with bright fruit and toasty oak as the price climbs.

In South Africa, New Zealand, and the Americas, producers who label their wine "Shiraz" are imitating the jazzy Australian style, which is typically aged in well-toasted oak, whereas those who use "Syrah" are after the more subtle French style with less obvious sweet oak influence. In these New World areas where the wines are varietally (rather than geographically) labeled, the more expensive the Syrah is, the more heavily oaked it is.

Australian Shiraz, especially from the excellent growing regions of Clare Valley, Eden Valley, McLaren Vale, Barossa Valley, and Hunter Valley is inky in color, with raspberry, boysenberry, lilac, lavender, menthol, and sweet vanilla (from oak aging) notes. Some even have notes of cinnamon raisin bagel or barbecue sauce. There is nothing shy or understated about these wines. They are outgoing, warm, friendly, and instantly likeable. Despite relatively high alcohol, generous oak usage, and sweet, ripe fruit, the better producers still aim for balance, often adding acidity back in during the winemaking process for freshness.

MUSICIAN

 It is rare that one artist can pull off being strong, bold, consistent, and reliable while at the same time showing a soft, vulnerable side, like Syrah/Shiraz. Pink is it. Her little spirit sister, Halsey, is waiting in the wings.

DATING PROFILE

- If I am French, I am shy and reluctant but worth seeking out.
- If I am from Australia, I am an open book—pleasant, friendly, and for the most part will go with the flow.
- Sometimes, I am spicy and sultry. Other times, I am as sweet as pie.
- While I am not as well loved as my rival Pinot Noir, I am less moody, more loyal, and very consistent. Date Pinot Noir. Then marry me.
- Like a fine perfume, I will show myself to you slowly over time.

SENSE EXERCISE

Spice Cabinet

Go to your kitchen spice shelf and take out whole peppercorns. Roll a small handful of them around the palm of your hand. Set down the peppercorns, then quickly smell your palm. Their oils are now on the top of your skin. Rinse off your hand and do the same with a green herb, such as thyme, rosemary, or oregano. The more you break down the leaves, the more aromatics you will sense. These are two of the elements you may come across in Syrah/Shiraz. Do you have a jar of bay leaves? They are aromatic enough to smell whole. Their light herbal/mint scent is similar to eucalyptus, native to Australia, so here is another element you can recognize, this time in Shiraz.

MATCHMAKING

Syrah/Shiraz is fairly easy to match with many types of dishes. It is reliably a medium to full-bodied dry red with bright red to dark berry fruit. Its other elements blend well with brown gravy, mustard, bacon, or game. As with most dry reds, keep fiery spices to a minimum. Syrah is rich enough, however, to play well with savory spices, such as complex Indian, Moroccan, or the more single-note star anise.

EVERY DAY WITH SYRAH/SHIRAZ

SYRAH

Braised pork loin

Cassoulet

Roasted root vegetables with thyme/Syrah sauce

Turkey and gravy

SHIRAZ

Chicken mole

Hoisin pork

Indian-spiced lamb stew

Beef short ribs (or tofu/tempeh/root vegetable) with garlic mustard sauce

Chili

INSTA DINNER

Marie Callender's—Swedish Meatballs

UPSCALE CONVENIENCE

Home Chef—Rib Eye Steak Stroganoff

SNACK

Lean Cuisine—Philly-Style Steak and Cheese Panini

CHEESE

Baked Brie

DINNER TONIGHT

BACON CHEESEBURGER

Serve with the light, tart, and fresh Faury Syrah, Collines Rhodaniennes $24.

BLACK BEAN HOISIN WRAPS

Serve with the full, supple, ripe, and jammy Wakefield Promised Land Shiraz, Clare Valley $13.

SHOPPING

It is hard to believe but finding a good Syrah/Shiraz at retail is harder than finding a good Chardonnay. Why? The popularity of Aussie Shiraz means that at entry-level pricing, there is going to be a wide variation in quality. As I've mentioned before, avoid the critter labels. There are the big brands and the little guys. Well-selected big brands are fine—see my picks here—but if there is someone on hand who had a say in the selection or is very passionate about Australian wines, ask for recommendations. Wine.com has online sommeliers to chat with, so you could start with a query about their favorite Australian reds at your desired price point.

As with other wines, the more specific the geography, likely the better the quality. For everyday enjoyment or entertaining large groups, I recommend the Jacob's Creek Shiraz Classic over many others from larger South Eastern Australia, a super zone made up of New South Wales, Victoria, Tasmania, part of Queensland, and part of South Australia. Even from the more specific areas, Australian wines dominate the under-$20 category.

Shopping for French Syrah is less of a minefield, as production is small and quality high across the board.

EVERYDAY VALUE/SHOPPING UNDER $20

France
Jean-Luc Colombo Syrah Les Collines de Laure, Collines Rhodaniennes $18
Lightly chewy, reserved, and dry with notes of cherry, black olive, blackened ahi, and forest floor

USA
Qupé Syrah, Central Coast $19
Velvety, then tart and dry, with notes of wild strawberry, cranberry, chocolate cherry, and plum skin

Chile
Natura Syrah, Valle Rapel $11
Silky, vibrant, and fresh with notes of cherry, boysenberry, blackberry, bay leaf, walnut, vanilla, and cedar (organically grown)

South Africa
Man Family Wines Shiraz, Coastal Region South Africa $12
Smooth, rich, dry, and earthy with notes of cherry, mulberry, mint, and eucalyptus

Australia
Jacob's Creek Shiraz Classic, South Eastern Australia $14
Smooth and supple with notes of boysenberry, plum, cocoa nib, black licorice, black pepper, and violet

Jim Barry The Lodge Hill Shiraz, Clare Valley $19
Full, supple, ripe, balanced with notes of cherry and blueberry pie, red rose, chocolate and vanilla ice cream, and mint

Hope Estate Shiraz Basalt Block, Hunter Valley $14
Rich and chewy with notes of blueberry, blackberry, vanilla, pecan, and nutmeg

Langmeil Hangin' Snakes Shiraz Viognier, Barossa $18
Round and lightly chewy with notes of cranberry, fig, sage, tarragon, cumin, and vanilla bean

Oxford Landing Estates Shiraz, South Australia $10
Lightly chewy, and fresh with notes of cherry, dark chocolate, vanilla, red licorice, and lavender

Wakefield Promised Land Shiraz, Clare Valley $13

> *Full, supple, ripe, and jammy with notes of blueberry, boysenberry, vanilla, and dark chocolate*

IMPRESS YOUR GUESTS/SHOPPING $20–$50

France

Faury Syrah, Collines Rhodaniennes $24

> *Light, tart, and fresh with notes of cranberry, raspberry, cherry, pink rose, lavender, and black peppercorn*

Vidal-Fleury, Crozes-Hermitage $25

> *Subtle and juicy with notes of blackberry, fig, violet, white rose, fennel, and cedar*

Jean-Michel Gerin, Saint-Joseph $32

> *Softly chewy with notes of cherry, grilled meat, black pepper, and black olives*

USA

Cadaretta Syrah, Columbia Valley, Washington $35

> *Full, round, and lusciously fruity with notes of berry pie, mint, black licorice, vanilla, and maple-smoked bacon*

Hess Collection Small Block Series Syrah Rosé, Napa Valley $22

> *Bone dry, racy, and bold with notes of raspberry, sour cherry, pomegranate, and white rose petal*

Bonny Doon Vineyard Syrah Le Pousseur, Central Coast $26

> *Feminine and perfumed with notes of raspberry, cherry, lilac, white and black pepper, savory herbs, and scrub and bacon*

Eberle Syrah Steinbeck Vineyard, Paso Robles $28

> *Supple, ripe, lightly chewy, and tart with notes of blueberry, boysenberry, red licorice, mint, white rose, cedar, and cinnamon*

Australia

John Duval Wines Entity Shiraz, Barossa $35

> *Bold and rich with notes of cherry, black licorice, black pepper, marjoram, cinnamon, chocolate, and beef jerky*

Penfolds Bin 28 Kalimna Shiraz, South Australia $30

> *Rich and chewy with notes of blueberry, blackberry, vanilla, pecan, and nutmeg*

Torbreck Woodcutter's Shiraz, Barossa Valley $24

> *Bold and spicy with notes of blackberry, spearmint, fruitcake, white pepper, and barnyard*

Wirra Wirra Catapult Shiraz, McLaren Vale $20

Lightly chewy and fresh with notes of pomegranate, cherry, menthol, thyme, and coffee bean

WORTH THE SPLURGE/SHOPPING $50 AND ABOVE

France

Jean-Luc Colombo, Cornas Terres Brûlées $57

Youthful and chewy with forward barrel notes of vanilla and toast along with cherry and browning mushrooms—decant or cellar

Delas Domaine des Tourettes, Hermitage $120

Softly chewy, silky, and fresh with notes of cranberry, raspberry, plum, black licorice, cedar, and dark roast coffee bean

E. Guigal, Côte-Rôtie Brune et Blonde $78

Youthful and very dry with notes of strawberry, cherry, plum, violet, lavender, and leather

USA

Bien Nacido Vineyards Syrah Estate, Santa Maria Valley $60

Rich, bold, and chewy with notes of peppercorn steak, black olive, violet, and dark chocolate

Dutton Goldfield Syrah Cherry Ridge, Green Valley of Russian River Valley $50

Full, lusciously ripe, fruity, and tart with notes of boysenberry, mulberry, blueberry, fig, and dark chocolate

Shafer Vineyards Relentless Syrah, Napa Valley $87

Rich, big-boned, supple, and gently chewy with notes of cherry, boysenberry, chocolate-covered raisin, pistachio, and vanilla

Australia

Penfolds St. Henri Shiraz, South Australia $99

Chewy, intense, and jammy with notes of raspberry, mulberry, cherry cola, mushroom, cinnamon, and clove

New Zealand

Trinity Hill Syrah Homage, Hawke's Bay $90

Soft and inviting with a fine, lightly chewy plum skin texture and notes of mulberry, cassis, sage, and vanilla

DINING OUT

Ordering French Syrah is not too demanding once you wrap your head around the vineyard area names, such as Côte-Rôtie or Crozes-Hermitage. Look for one of the village or vineyard names mentioned here, check the price, and then ask the wine person or sommelier for his or her recommendation. Some outstanding but harder-to-find producers include Jean-Louis Chave, Jamet, Jasmin, and Rostaing.

When it comes to the Australian or American versions, brands are much more important, so here again, ask for recommendations and give the sommelier both price parameters and stylistic preferences. For a nice nonverbal communication of target price, run your finger across the wine list page, point to a price you like, and say, "We'd like something in this range." If you'd like to try one of the best and price is no object, ask for Henschke Hill of Grace, or Penfolds Grange.

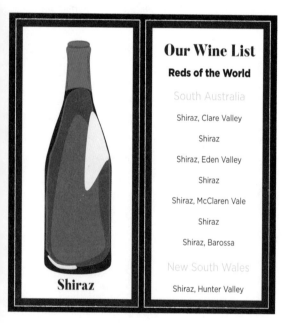

Shiraz

Our Wine List

Reds of the World

South Australia

Shiraz, Clare Valley

Shiraz

Shiraz, Eden Valley

Shiraz

Shiraz, McClaren Vale

Shiraz

Shiraz, Barossa

New South Wales

Shiraz, Hunter Valley

BRANCH OUT

GRENACHE

Grenache is often blended with Syrah to plump it up and add pleasant strawberry fruit. Grenache is the main player in Côtes du Rhône wines, which are a great value. Grenache-based wines are delicious and easygoing enough to enjoy as a cocktail and to serve at parties. I used to call Grenache George Hamilton, the actor who was always smiling and tanned. Today I call Grenache Justin Bieber.

Bonny Doon Vineyard Clos du Gilroy Grenache, Monterey, California $20
> *Mediterranean-style fruity and tart Grenache with notes of raspberry jam, white pepper, and dried herbs*

Chapoutier Belleruche, Côtes-du-Rhône $17
> *Silky, fresh, tart, and dry with notes of blueberry, mulberry, boysenberry, tarragon, and basil*

Check Your Success Quiz

1. Is Syrah the same grape as Shiraz? Yes/No
2. Côte-Rôtie is like rotisserie chicken in that the hillside (*côte*) is "roasted" by the sun. True/False

---

QUE SIRAH SYRAH

Petite Sirah from California is lip-smacking, juicy, jammy, sometimes peppery, and often heavily oaked. The classic example of this is the Stags' Leap Petite Sirah, Napa Valley $45. Folks often think Petite Sirah is nearly identical to Syrah, but it has no relation whatsoever. It is simply an American name for the French grape Durif.

8

MERLOT

Merlot is as easy to say as it is to enjoy. Smooth, supple, fruity, and inviting, this suave little number is just the ticket for those who find red wine
superstar Cabernet Sauvignon too rich, robust, and chewy, especially
those from the USA. As Merlot's popularity soared in the 1990s, so did
its prices, and along the way the market was flooded with a lot of mediocre wines, surprisingly more so at the upper end. I remember writing a column
on Napa Valley Merlot for which I tasted over 100 wines at price ranges from $20
to $150. My lowest-rated wines were categorically those over $100.

Then came the movie *Sideways* in 2004, which introduced a new generation of
wine drinkers to Pinot Noir. Merlot sales dropped dramatically, overtaken with
the new "it" wine. Thankfully, these days Merlot is back, stronger, and more com-
petitive, with quality higher than ever (for the most part).

HISTORY

During the 1850s, Merlot was planted on both sides of the Gironde estuary in
Bordeaux—and along its tributaries, the Garonne and the Dordogne—and in
Veneto, Italy, but its success at that time was most notable in the Libourne, on the
right bank of the Dordogne. To this day, Libournais villages Pomerol and, to a
lesser extent, Saint-Émilion produce the most highly prized Merlot wines in the
world. As it ripens earlier than Cabernet Sauvignon, it is a favorite juicy snack for
the local blackbird, or *merle*, for which it is said to be named. DNA testing shows
that Merlot's parents are Cabernet Franc and Magdeleine Noire des Charentes.
This makes it a half-sibling to Cabernet Sauvignon, whose parents are Cabernet
Franc and Sauvignon Blanc.

GEOGRAPHY

Merlot is the most widely planted grape in Bordeaux, France. In the Médoc, to the west along the Atlantic coast, where Cabernet Sauvignon is the star, its earlier ripening ability makes it reliably part of the team, providing up to 40 percent of the blend. An exception in the Médoc is the southerly, cooler village of Margaux, whose wines are typically 60 percent and higher Merlot. Heat-loving Cabernet Sauvignon struggles even more here than in the northern riverside vineyards.

It is in the cool soils of the right bank to the east, particularly in Pomerol (think: Pomerlot) and in Saint-Émilion, that Merlot produces a reliable crop of red-fruited, thin-skinned grapes. The blending partner here is Cabernet Franc, which is as little as 5 percent of the blends in Pomerol to as much as 60 percent in Saint-Émilion, depending on weather and vineyard location. Local producers Christian Moueix and Michel Rolland, who consult around the globe, are known as the "Merlot masters" or the "kings of Merlot."

The world's most expensive wine, named after a single pine tree near the winery, Château Le Pin, is a Merlot-based wine from Pomerol starting at around $2,000. Château Pétrus is another big name. Prices rise steeply as collectors vie for one of the rare cases or bottles. Their rarity factor and the hunt for the trophy are what drive prices way above market value, just as they do with modernist, cult producers, called *garagistes* for their artisanal, small-scale operations. While they are lovely wines, I find these modernist styles less interesting than those of the traditional producers. Vieux Château Certan is one of my favorites, though this is still about $350 for a current release. Luckily, many reasonably priced wines are available for under $100. If $20 is more in line for a weeknight wine, Lalande-de-Pomerol and Montagne-St-Émilion are excellent satellite areas to plumb, as are wines from Côtes de Bordeaux Cadillac, south of the city of Bordeaux, and wines called Bordeaux Supérieur, produced with grapes grown anywhere in Bordeaux.

Merlot has a long history in Italy. It is widely planted in Friuli-Venezia Giulia in the north, as well as in Umbria, Abruzzo, and Tuscany in central Italy. Italian Merlot recently has garnered global attention as Masseto, from the Frescobaldi family's Masseto hill overlooking the Mediterranean Sea in Bolgheri in southern Tuscany. This Super Tuscan Merlot gets fully ripe, giving that smooth, supple, mouth-filling quality that is so appealing, yet with balancing underlying acidity for freshness. Masseto is $700 for a current release, and like Château Le Pin, is snapped up by trophy-hunting collectors. Not to worry. I will recommend a few more realistically priced versions.

In North America, the best Merlots come from sunny California and Washington's arid, sunny Columbia Valley and its subregions, including Walla Walla Valley. In South America, Chilean Merlot, grown there in proximity to Cabernet Sauvignon in the coastal valleys south of Santiago, is worth seeking out. It also plays along as a blending partner with Cabernet in Bordeaux-style wines.

MERLOT AT A GLANCE

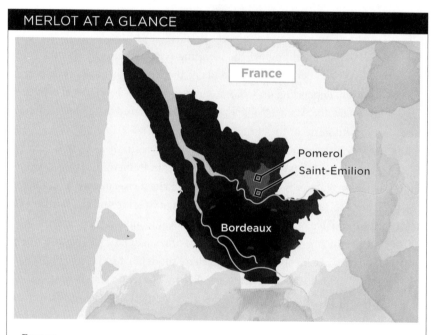

France:

- Bordeaux: Pomerol, Lalande-de-Pomerol, Saint-Émilion, Montagne-St-Émilion, Côtes de Bordeaux Cadillac, Bordeaux Supérieur

Italy:

- Friuli-Venezia Giulia
- Tuscany: Bolgheri
- Umbria
- Abruzzo

USA: California, Washington

Chile

TASTE PROFILE AND STYLES

Château Le Pin, the benchmark for Merlot, is big, powerful, and brooding, with layers of rich extract and firm but fine texture. It ages extremely well, showing an intensity of raspberry and cherry fruit and even softer, finer texture than a red Burgundy, the archetype of silky wine. Pomerols are typically ethereal, soft, rich, and earthy. Saint-Émilions, of which Château Cheval Blanc is the ultimate, tend to have a slightly firmer texture, especially when young. The best of both Pomerol and Saint-Émilion require aging. Simpler Merlots are ready to enjoy right away. Northern Italian Merlot is light and tart with notes of cherry and often black licorice, whereas those from the warmer center of Italy are richer, plusher, but still offer freshness and finesse.

California Merlots are often described as "chocolate-covered cherry," but I like to describe them as Neapolitan ice cream, as there is lavish vanilla from oak barrels added to the mix. In Washington's Columbia Valley and its subzones, the Merlots are very rich and sweetly fruited with a unique blueberry-mocha note. Many are aged in American oak barrels, which can bring notes of coconut or dill as well as grip and chewiness. Chilean Merlot is popularly priced, found in grocery and discount stores. Use my buying guide on the following pages to find the more interesting wines, which are supple, flavorful, elegant, and nicely balanced.

SENSE EXERCISE

Multidimensional Learning

Let's try experiential multidimensional learning, a.k.a. drinking the wine from a region while looking at a map of that region. This works best with at least four people. First, assign each participant a region to bring a wine from—Lalande-de-Pomerol, Montagne-St-Émilion, Margaux, and Bordeaux Supérieur.

Provide a cheese board. Print out or display a large map of the wine regions of Bordeaux, which you can find here:

Bordeaux.com/us/Our-Terroir/The-Medoc
Bordeaux.com/us/Our-Terroir/The-Libournais

Then, it's off to the races. As you compare the wines, look closely at their regional names and they will become more familiar to you.

MUSICIAN

 John Legend's voice is smooth, mellow, warming, and calming, one that everybody knows, like a nice glass of Merlot.

DATING PROFILE

- I show my softer side quickly.
- I am straightforward and easy to get along with.
- You can take me anywhere. I am known around the world.
- I will stay with you, by your side.
- At my best I am very, very expensive.

KING OF MERLOT: CHRISTIAN MOUEIX

Excerpted from my Sommelier Journal *interview:*

As I pulled into the parking lot of Dominus in Yountville, California, I couldn't help but notice the difference between this discreet, nearly invisible structure and the many architectural showcases along Highway 29. I had already learned that French winemakers weren't driven by ego. Still, when Christian Moueix came walking down the long driveway to greet me, I felt like one of the chosen few.

This scorching June afternoon fell right in the middle of the frenzied 2009 Bordeaux futures campaign, and it was the day after France had been eliminated from the World Cup. The hours whizzed by as Moueix answered my questions, poured wine for tasting, and showed me around the vineyards. It quickly became clear that this brilliant, passionate man was also extremely humble, hospitable, and precise. Never one to miss a detail, he even offered to return to the winery to get me a cold bottle of water after walking me back to my car.

Moueix is best known as the manager of Château Pétrus and proprietor of other legendary Bordeaux estates, but he became enthralled with Northern California during his studies at the University of California, Davis, in the late 1960s. After a long search for a site to call his own, he got the opportunity to buy into the historic Napanook property west of Yountville in 1982, signing an agreement with Robin Lail and Marcia Smith, the daughters of original owner John Daniel. The first harvest for Dominus was 1983;

a second label, Napanook, was launched in 1996. Moueix became the sole proprietor in 1995. Meanwhile, he continues to manage the family firm in France, as he has done since his father, Jean-Pierre, retired in 1990.

CF: How would you describe the role of Château Pétrus in raising public and critical estimation of the Right Bank?

CM: I may not be in the best position to answer. I was in charge of Pétrus for my family between 1970 and 2008. Since 2008, my brother, Jean-François, and a young man, Olivier Berrouet, have been in charge, and I act as a consultant. I would say Pétrus has been key for the Merlot varietal more than for the Right Bank. Merlot became extremely popular in the '80s and the '90s, and it was really helped, I would say, by Pomerol, by the fame of Château Pétrus itself. The fame of Merlot was partly destroyed by that stupid movie *Sideways*, but it was a good lesson for me. Any reputation can be destroyed by something unexpected. Château Pétrus was not directly affected by that movie, but my basic Merlot that I used to sell in the States—about 1 million cases all told—was almost destroyed by that movie. It had been $8.99 on the shelf for many years, and with the film, the sales plummeted. That was one more lesson of modesty. So Pétrus was a star for the Right Bank, together with Cheval Blanc or Figeac or Ausone or other famous châteaux, but in general, the role of Pétrus was to raise awareness of Merlot.

MATCHMAKING

Merlot pairs nicely with earthy flavors found in meats, vegetables, and cheeses. As with most dry reds, avoid richly spiced foods.

EVERY DAY WITH MERLOT

Hamburger steak with brown gravy

Barbecued chicken

Rack of lamb

Coq au vin (chicken in Merlot sauce)

Salmon à la plancha

Grilled eggplant on rustic bread

Cremini omelet

Quinoa paprika black bean bowl

Vegetable kebabs

Wild mushroom risotto

CHEESE

Fontina at its best is earthy, fruity, and nutty, delicious with an Italian or French Merlot

INSTA DINNER

Lean Cuisine—Beef Pot Roast

Evol—Truffle Parmesan & Portobella Risotto

UPSCALE CONVENIENCE

Sun Basket—Languedoc-Style Pork with Pecan Aillade and Braised Greens

SNACK

MEXICAN THREE-CHEESE QUESADILLA

Use the earthy, buttery V&V Supremo blend of Chihuahua brand, Oaxaca, and Cotija cheeses or the milder Kraft or Sargento blends.

DINNER TONIGHT

LENTIL AND HAM SOUP

Lentils cook in about 20 minutes. Add celery, carrot, onion, and seasonings to taste. A ham hock or leg can give flavor, and ham chunks or sausage slices added at the end give richness. Vegetarians: replace the meat with mushrooms, tofu, or tempeh. Serve with the pleasantly fruity and supple Ferrari-Carano Merlot, Sonoma County $21, or the light and supple Château Belle-Graves, Lalande-de-Pomerol $18.

SHOPPING

EVERYDAY VALUE/SHOPPING UNDER $20

France

Mouton Cadet Rosé, Bordeaux $11

> *Light, dry, fresh, and mellow Merlot-based wine with notes of lemon zest, wild strawberry, and wintergreen*

Château Belle-Graves, Lalande-de-Pomerol $18

> *Light and supple with notes of cherry, cedar, mushroom, and salami*

Château de Fontenille, Cadillac Côtes de Bordeaux $18

> *Delicate, soft, gently chewy, and fresh with notes of cherry, plum, bay leaf, rose petal, and milk chocolate*

USA

Bogle Vineyards Merlot, California $9

Smooth, dry, and complex with notes of blackberry, plum, fig, black olive, vanilla, dark chocolate, and espresso

Kendall-Jackson Avant Red Blend, California $17

Like a riper Beaujolais, this Merlot/Syrah-based blend is light, juicy, and dry with notes of strawberry, cherry, cassis, black pepper, and pink rose (certified renewable energy)

Horse Heaven Hills H3 Merlot, Heaven Hills, Columbia Valley $15

Medium-bodied and smooth with notes of dark cherry, blueberry, vanilla bean, and nutmeg

Chile

Cono Sur Merlot, Chile $12

Soft, dry, and lightly chewy with notes of plum and Bing cherry

Cousiño Macul Merlot, Maipo Valley $11

Full and supple with notes of blackberry, blueberry, cinnamon, caraway, and cacao nib

IMPRESS YOUR GUESTS/SHOPPING $20-$50

France

Château Dubourg, Saint–Émilion $20

Light, finely chewy, and dry with notes of cherry, graphite, and cedar

Folie de Chauvin, Saint-Émilion $26

Dry and lightly gripping with notes of cherry, cassis, fig, mushroom, maple, and cedar

Château Simard, Grand Cru, Saint-Émilion $48

Lightly chewy, fresh, and elegant Merlot blend with notes of cherry, sun-dried tomato, roasted eggplant, mushroom, and cedar

Château de Parenchère Cuvée Raphaël, Bordeaux Supérieur $21

Plush, then lightly chewy Merlot blend with notes of raspberry, cassis, plum, vanilla, nutmeg, and espresso

Italy

Conte Brandolini d'Adda Vistorta, Friuli Grave $23

Midweight, tart, pithy, and dry Italian Merlot with notes of dark cherry, black licorice, spearmint, fennel seed, orange peel, and espresso

Masciarelli Marina Cvetic Merlot, Terre Aquilane, Abruzzo $25

Supple, juicy, and fresh with notes of fig tart, mulberry, blueberry, plum, and very dark chocolate

USA

Charles Krug Merlot, Napa Valley $24

Inviting, full, plush, then lightly chewy with notes of fig, plum, caramelized mushroom, vanilla, and cocoa

Clos Pegase Merlot Mitsuko's Vineyard, Carneros, Napa Valley $40

Rich and round with notes of plum, raisin, date, dark roast coffee, molasses, and dark chocolate

Dry Creek Vineyard Merlot, Dry Creek Valley $26

Full, supple, complex, and very nicely balanced with notes of cherry cola, cassis, mulberry, vanilla bean, and espresso

Ferrari-Carano Merlot, Sonoma $21

Full, supple, tart, and clean with notes of raspberry, cassis, plum, and chocolate-covered raisin

Gundlach Bundschu Merlot, Sonoma Valley $35

Juicy, balanced, supple, and flavorful with notes of cassis, mulberry, mocha, mint, and Fig Newton

Provenance Vineyards Merlot, Napa Valley $40

Rich and plush with notes of cherry cobbler, blackberry, plum skin, fennel seed, tobacco, and vanilla

Rombauer Vineyards Merlot, Carneros, Napa Valley $35

Soft, supple, and earthy with notes of black currant, plum, tomato, butternut squash, and coffee bean

DaMa Merlot, Walla Walla Valley $35

Plush, ripe, and softly textured with notes of blueberry, cassis, cherry, vanilla bean, and cedar

L'Ecole No 41 Estate Merlot, Walla Walla $36

Full and lightly chewy with notes of blueberry, fennel seed, cigar box, vanilla, and coffee bean

WORTH THE SPLURGE/SHOPPING $50 AND ABOVE

France

Château Beauregard, Pomerol $65

Soft and gentle with a very fine peach skin chewiness and layers of cherry, cassis, braised meats, cumin, and cedar

Château Clinet, Pomerol $89

Very elegant and intense with notes of cherry, fig, graphite, and truffle

Château Lafleur-Gazin, Pomerol $54

Inviting, fine, and slightly chewy with notes of plum, graphite, forest floor, leaf pile, and tobacco

Château Le Bon Pasteur, Pomerol $99

Elegant and supple with notes of plum, cassis, vanilla, cedar, sage, moss, and graphite

Château du Tertre, Margaux $50

Concentrated, bright, and chewy with notes of black currant, sweet cherry, chicory, cigar box, and earth

USA

Darioush Merlot, Napa Valley $58

Ripe, velvety, and oaky with notes of berry compote, coffee bean, mocha, and caramel

Duckhorn Vineyards Merlot, Napa Valley $54

Supple, then very lightly chewy with notes of raspberry tart, vanilla bean, chocolate mint, and dark roast coffee

Shafer Vineyards Merlot, Napa Valley $55

Big, rich, and initially creamy with a juicy core of black cherry, cherry cola, plum, black olive, cedar, pinecone, and vanilla—iconic Napa Valley Merlot; cellar worthy

St. Supéry Merlot Rutherford Estate, Napa Valley $50

Soft, inviting, full-bodied, and lightly oaked with notes of mulberry, boysenberry, forest floor, and cigar box; very finely textured and exquisitely balanced

Pepper Bridge Merlot, Walla Walla Valley $50

Supple, lusciously fruity, and slightly oaky with notes of blackberry, boysenberry, blueberry, cedar, cinnamon, vanilla, and mocha

DINING OUT

The best French Merlots are going to be pricey. This is a good time to go out into satellite areas for similar styles, if perhaps slightly less complex. Keep in mind, too, that these simpler wines are often ready to drink right upon release, so they are a slam dunk in this regard as well. Look to Lalande-de-Pomerol, Montagne-St-Émilion, and Bordeaux Supérieur in particular. Wines from Margaux are good bets as well. While Château Margaux is the considered the best, and is priced to reflect its position as a collector's wine, look for wines from the village of Margaux, such as Château du Tertre.

Italian Merlot is a minefield. It is so popular already, and will beat the com-

Our Wine List

Reds of the World

Merlot

Merlot, Pomerol

Merlot, Lalande-de-Pomerol

Merlot

Merlot, St. Émilion

Merlot, Montagne-St.-Émilion

Merlot

Merlot, Côtes de Bordeaux
Cadillac

Merlot

Merlot, Bordeaux Supérieur

Merlot

petition on price. Order one of my recommended wines, or really engage the sommelier. Show him or her this shopping section, and ask for something similar if the restaurant doesn't have the exact wine.

The same can be said of North and South American Merlots. Stick with the better red wine areas in Central Chile south of Santiago—Maipo in particular. In California, Sonoma Merlots, such as the Dry Creek Vineyard or Ferrari-Carano, are often half the price of their Napa Valley counterparts. Stay away from grocery store brands and ask the sommelier to recommend smaller producers from California and from Washington.

BRANCH OUT

Argentine Malbec is as fruity, inviting, and softly textured as Merlot, if less earthy and slightly fuller in body. Try the beautifully balanced and well-priced Zuccardi Serie A Malbec, Valle de Uco $15, or the lusciously ripe and fruity Susana Balbo Signature Malbec, Mendoza $25.

Check Your Success Quiz
1. The most expensive Merlot in the world is named after a _____ tree.
2. Pomerol is a world-class Merlot-producing region in California. True/False

9

CABERNET SAUVIGNON

Cabernet Sauvignon is the king of the wine world. If light, sweet, juicy White Zinfandel represents the palate starting point, this robust, chewy red is its final destination. The Brits and their love affair with Claret (Cabernet blends from Bordeaux, France) drove its popularity to a global level even before Robert Parker "discovered" it in 1982. There is something immediately recognizable, too, even in the simplest versions. It is like running into an old friend. Cabernet Sauvignon is planted, and well received, all over the world.

HISTORY

In eighteenth-century France, the Médoc area of Bordeaux was widely planted with both Petite and Grand Vidure, or little and big "hard-wooded vine." Later on, Grand Vidure was referred to as Carménère, and Petite Vidure was referred to as Cabernet Sauvignon. Thanks to UC Davis DNA testing, we now know that Cabernet Sauvignon is in fact the offspring of Cabernet Franc and Sauvignon Blanc. It is easy to smell and taste this, as less ripe Cabernet Sauvignons offer up a little zesty green or herbaceous note of Sauvignon Blanc, whereas the pretty red berry fruit of Cabernet Franc comes through as well. If you've ever had a Kir, you can relate—adding crème de cassis (black currant liqueur) to a light, tart, even sour white wine makes for a delicious, refreshing combination.

GEOGRAPHY

Cabernet Sauvignon likes it hot. Not too hot, but much hotter than, say, Pinot Noir or Chardonnay. It thrives in moderately warm climates around the world. In cool climates, it requires warm, gravelly soil that doesn't stay wet. Other than that, it is easygoing and reliable, and produces a loose cluster of thick-skinned grapes with a large seed, or pip, giving a very concentrated, inky, chewy, and flavorful juice.

The complexities of Bordeaux, Cabernet Sauvignon's benchmark producing area in France, are great. It is one of the most difficult wine areas to sort out. Much of the intense theory here is based on classification, or ranking systems, which are not so important when beginning to learn about wine. What is important, as in other Old World areas, is basic geography. This great grape deserves your attention, whether ultimately you like it or you don't. It is important to at least dip one's toes in the water. (After all, *bordeaux* means "border of the water"!)

Bordeaux is a vast region producing dry white and sweet white wines as well as its blue-chip reds. The weather is not ideal for ripening the heat-loving Cabernet Sauvignon, so other grapes are planted and allowed to be blended in at the winemaker's discretion. These grapes—Merlot, Cabernet Franc, Malbec, and Petit Verdot, along with Cabernet Sauvignon—make up the Bordeaux family. Each brings something to the party. Think of these grapes as the Golden State Warriors, for instance. Steph Curry is dope, but if he has a broken ankle, can the team still win? Absolutely. The players work as a team. Having early-ripening, plush, and velvety Merlot on the Bordeaux team is especially important, as it smooths out the rough edges and plumps up the fruit. Cabernet Franc adds appealing red berry notes.

Cabernet Sauvignon is site sensitive and heat-loving, so it is planted in the gravelly riverbanks of the Médoc, a sliver of land jutting upward from the city of Bordeaux, bordered to the west by the chilly, stormy Atlantic, and to the east by the calmer and more serene Gironde estuary. I have sailed both bodies of water on a medium-size cruise ship as a wine guest lecturer. It is easy to imagine Bordeaux-laden vessels sailing up the Gironde and out into the Atlantic toward London. How everything is fine, and the voyage is smooth. Then, upon entering the rough Atlantic, everyone starts getting seasick. It is here that the ship I was on had lost a baby grand in the early days, before such heavy items were bolted down.

From the Atlantic dunes inward, storm-buffering forests transition to inland, flat former marshlands, and then finally, right at the bank of the Gironde, well-draining, warm gravelly soils. It is here, in Saint-Estèphe, Pauillac, Saint-Julien, and Margaux, where one can skip stones on the river, that the most highly ranked, or classified Cabernets come from. They are referred to as growths, as in how a plant grows, or where they grow—the vineyard, or cru.

The French have given the great classed growths, or Grand Cru Classe, five levels, or classifications to the Médoc wines. First (or best) Growths Château Lafite-Rothschild, Château Latour, and Château Mouton Rothschild are all in the village of Pauillac. Château Margaux, in Margaux, is the last one in the Médoc proper,

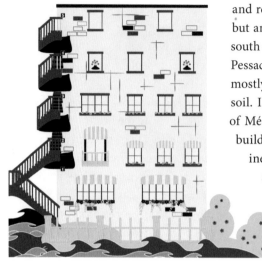

and remember this is Merlot-dominant, but another, Château Haut-Brion, is just south of the city of Bordeaux in protected Pessac-Léognan, part of Graves, which is mostly a suburb named after its gravelly soil. I like to think of the classification of Médoc wines as a five-story walk-up building. The best products are prominently displayed on the first floor, showing their superior rank. The lower the ranking, the farther away the wines are placed. You can also think of it as orchestra vs. stratosphere seats in a theater.

"Cru Bourgeois" is another term, not an official ranking, though, applied toward more everyday-priced wines than the Classified Growths. This name stems from the Middle Ages, when inhabitants of the "bourg" of Bordeaux, a working-class village, were given special privileges, including exemption from taxes on the sale of their wines during English rule. As commerce grew they took their profits and bought up some of the best vineyard sites (*crus*) in the area.

Within the Médoc is the Haut-Médoc, covering all but the northern reaches near the mouth of the estuary. Within the Haut-Médoc are from north to south the riverside villages of Saint-Estèphe, Pauillac, Saint-Julien, and Margaux. Margaux is the coolest and tends to have 60 percent or more Merlot rather than that base of Cabernet Sauvignon. South of the city is Graves.

Going beyond Bordeaux, the Sud de France is a source of well-priced everyday Cabernet Sauvignons and the grape name is right on the label.

Cabernet Sauvignon is well loved in Italy, where the quality ranges from straightforward, everyday drinking to the most serious Super Tuscan wine, Sassicaia. It thrives in warm Mediterranean Tuscany and on the nearby isle of Sardinia.

In California's Napa Valley north of San Francisco, robust, chewy, and super-ripe Cabernet Sauvignon has become a global benchmark. Sonoma versions are often softer and suppler, a style prized by Tom Jordan of Jordan Vineyard & Winery there, a Francophile who suffered an ulcer and couldn't tolerate robust wines. Remote and off-the-beaten-path Lake County in Northern California is a treasure

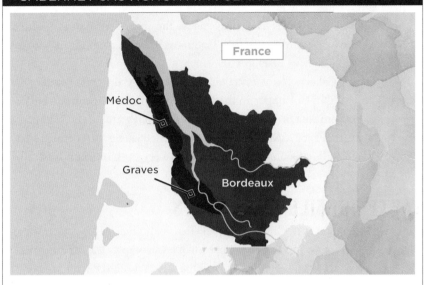

France:

- Bordeaux
  - Médoc: Haut-Médoc
    - Saint-Estèphe, Pauillac, Saint-Julien
  - Graves: Pessac-Léognan
- Sud de France

Italy: Tuscany, Sardinia

USA:

- California: Lake County, Napa Valley, Sonoma, Paso Robles
- Washington: Columbia Valley

Chile:

- Aconcagua: Maipo
- Valle Central: Colchagua

Argentina:

- Mendoza: Luján de Cuyo
- Salta: Cafayate, Calchaqui

Australia: South Australia: Coonawarra, Clare Valley

trove of ripe, balanced, juicy, and under-$20 Cabernet Sauvignon. In Paso Robles on the Central Coast, the identifying marker is velvety texture. Producers there say Napa Cabs have the velvet as often as you see the green flash at sunset, whereas Paso Cabs always have it. Washington's Columbia Valley is a significant source of rich, ripe, oaked Cabernet Sauvignons.

High-quality Cabernet Sauvignons are produced in Maipo, just south of Santiago in Chile, and in Colchagua in the Valle Central there. Argentina's Luján de Cuyo, or Little Bordeaux, in Mendoza, is a fine producing area, as is Calchaqui in Salta to the north. From Australia, the best Cabernet Sauvignons come from the terra rossa (red soil) of Coonawarra, and Clare Valley, both in South Australia.

TASTE PROFILE AND STYLES

Cabernet Sauvignon is medium- to full-bodied with notes of black currant and green bell pepper when less ripe, plus leather and earth in Bordeaux. In the New World, the fruit is riper, the alcohol higher, and thus the wine is more plush or softer in texture. Rich oak treatment provides extra layers of chewiness, grip, and flavor.

For many, the Cabernet Sauvignon benchmark is Napa Valley, where the grape thrives, especially at the hottest place there—the "pinch" in the hourglass—where the mountains are closest together near St. Helena. Those from Columbia Valley in Washington have trademark blueberry and mocha notes and lavish oak treatment.

The best Bordeaux wines are taut, chewy, gripping and even astringent while young and take years to reach a good drinking window, whereas the opposite is true of Napa Valley versions. Either way, straightforward Cabernet Sauvignon is an approachable combination of black currant or cassis fruit along with baking spices from the oak barrel with a little graphite and leather added in to the Bordeaux equation. It is not a complicated mix.

Cabernet Sauvignon is at its best rich, dense, chewy, recognizable and satisfying, the ultimate wine. To soften for earlier drinking, splash it into a carafe or pitcher and swirl it around. Then, serve in large-bowled glasses. Dishwasher-friendly stemless glasses are fine.

SENSE EXERCISE

Isolating Flavors

Grape jam is easy to find. Black currant, not so much. It is well worth it to find some and try it on toast as an exercise to build your descriptor toolbox for Cabernet Sauvignon. Cost Plus World Market has it, along with black currant hard candies, and violet candy while you are there. And licorice. And bay leaf. Isolating the flavor without the interference of wine is essential in building your recognition skills. You can do it!

MATCHMAKING

Bordeaux and lamb is a classic pairing, the earthiness and gamey notes melding into sweet black currant and leather, the rich texture smoothing the chewiness of the wine. This is a match made in heaven. California is earning a reputation for new classic pairings, one of which is Sonoma lamb with Sonoma Cabernet Sauvignon. Toss in a little mint jelly and you pick up on the minty, bay leaf, eucalyptus, fennel seed, or green olive notes found in some New World Cabernet Sauvignons.

The rich, bold flavor, chewiness, and palate grip of Cabernet Sauvignon works easily with well-marbled meats. Leaving meat aside, vegetarian options abound, especially if you introduce char or grilling. The key here is to have a juicy richness from the addition of olive oil, flaxseed oil, walnuts, or another fat source to soften the chewiness and grip of the wine.

EVERY DAY WITH CABERNET SAUVIGNON

London broil/flank steak

Tri tip

Beef brisket

Beef empanada/meat pie

Blue cheese burger

Roast leg of lamb

Rack of lamb

Grilled lamb chops

Grilled vegetable kebabs

Black bean burgers

INSTA DINNER

Lean Cuisine—Meatloaf with Mashed Potatoes

Lean Cuisine—Steak Portabella

Takeout—Baba ghanoush

UPSCALE CONVENIENCE

Blue Apron—Seared Beef Medallions with Roasted Broccoli and Rosemary Pan Sauce

SNACK

Gouda sliders or Gouda fondue

DINNER TONIGHT

SLOW COOKER ROAST BEEF OR VEGGIES

Set the ingredients in before work and come home to tender, succulent bites and tasty sips of the delicious and approachable Shooting Star Cabernet Sauvignon, Lake County $15, or the gently chewy and dry Château Larose-Trintaudon Cru Bourgeois, Haut-Médoc $25.

SHOPPING

EVERYDAY VALUE/SHOPPING UNDER $20

France

Les Hauts de Lagarde, Bordeaux $13

Lightly chewy, grippy, lean, and tart with notes of dark cherry, plum, cassis, graphite, and charred pepper (organically grown)

La Chevalière Cabernet Sauvignon, Pays d'Oc, Sud de France $13

Round and fruity with notes of cherry, mulberry, and blueberry

La Marouette Cabernet Sauvignon, Pays d'Oc, Sud de France $14

Sunny, plump, and easygoing, with notes of cassis, black cherry, black coffee, and mint (organically grown)

USA

Shooting Star Cabernet Sauvignon, Lake County $15

Nearly full-bodied and chewy with notes of cassis, blackberry, vanilla, toast, and mint

Buried Cane Cabernet Sauvignon, Columbia Valley $16

Supple and slightly chewy with notes of cherry, blueberry, plum, cassis, dried herbs, aged Sumatran coffee beans, and vanilla

Chile

Cousiño Macul Cabernet Sauvignon, Maipo Valley $11

Supple, fresh, and dry with notes of plum, cedar, sage, and cigar box

Veramonte Cabernet Sauvignon, Colchagua Valley $12

Lightly chewy, dry, and bright with notes of cassis, plum, dark chocolate, dark roast coffee, and vanilla

Argentina

Crios Cabernet Sauvignon, Mendoza $15

Fruity and supple with notes of black cherry, blackberry, black olive, and vanilla

La Linda Cabernet Sauvignon, Luján de Cuyo, Mendoza $12

Lightly chewy and fresh with notes of cassis, black olive, sage, coffee bean, and cocoa

Salentein Cabernet Sauvignon, Valle de Uco, Mendoza $19

Midweight and lightly chewy with notes of cherry, plum, cassis, red licorice, cedar, and vanilla

Australia

Wakefield Cabernet Sauvignon Promised Land, South Australia $13

Plush, lightly chewy, and fresh with notes of black cherry, cassis, sage, bay leaf, tobacco, nutmeg, and clove

IMPRESS YOUR GUESTS/SHOPPING $20-$50

France

Château Aney Cru Bourgeois, Haut-Médoc $36

Medium-bodied and chewy with notes of cherry, cassis, rhubarb, tomato paste, leather, graphite, cedar, and pipe smoke

Château Bernadotte, Haut-Médoc $25

Classic Bordeaux with notes of black currant, plum, cherry, tomato leaf, tobacco, leather, graphite, cedar, and vanilla

Château de Chantegrive, Pessac-Léognan, Graves $20

Classic red Graves, an equal blend of Cabernet Sauvignon and Merlot with notes of cherry, cassis, red rose, tobacco, and the area's signature dusty tannins

Château Larose-Trintaudon Cru Bourgeois, Haut Médoc $25

Gently chewy and dry with notes of cassis, fig, maple, cedar, sage, and black pepper

Château Patache d'Aux Cru Bourgeois, Médoc $25

Lightly chewy, fresh, and dry with notes of cherry, leather, white mushroom, and cedar

USA

Isabel Rosé of Cabernet Sauvignon, California $20

Crisp, clean, dry, and bracing with notes of citrus, cantaloupe, kiwi, strawberry, and sage; the black currant note reminds me of a Kir

Mount Veeder Winery Cabernet Sauvignon, Napa Valley $44

Full, layered, fruity, and oaky with a balancing freshness and notes of dark cherry, cherry cola, cassis, fennel sausage, green olive, cedar, and vanilla

Raymond Reserve Cabernet Sauvignon, Napa Valley $44

Very elegant, supple, and understated style with notes of plum skin, cassis, vanilla, and coffee bean and a gentle, fine, fresh texture

Sequoia Grove Cabernet Sauvignon, Napa Valley $38

Clean, fruit forward, and slightly gripping with notes of black cherry, plum, cassis, and vanilla; smooths out nicely with food

Terra Valentine Cabernet Sauvignon, Napa Valley $36

Polished, inviting, and velvety with notes of cherry, cassis, rosebud, mint chocolate, pipe tobacco, and vanilla bean

Two Iron Cabernet Sauvignon, Napa Valley $45

Full-bodied, rich, vibrant and expressive with notes of cherry, cassis, fig, dark chocolate, espresso, and sage leaf; lightly chewy and gripping

Beringer Cabernet Sauvignon, Knights Valley $34

Youthfully gripping with lush notes of cassis, black olive, vanilla, and cigar box

Louis M. Martini Cabernet Sauvignon, Sonoma $20

Light and chewy with notes of cherry, black currant, black olive, blackened ahi, cedar, and cumin

Stonestreet Estate Vineyards Cabernet Sauvignon, Alexander Valley $45

Full, soft, round, and fresh with notes of cherry cola, cassis, mocha, and coffee bean

Eberle Cabernet Sauvignon Estate, Paso Robles $45

Full and gently gripping with notes of black cherry, blueberry, bay leaf, fennel seed, red licorice, vanilla, and mocha

Justin Cabernet Sauvignon, Paso Robles $26

Opulent and lightly chewy with notes of currant, fig, raisin, dark chocolate, bay leaf, cinnamon, and clove

Rabble Mossfire Ranch Cabernet Sauvignon, Paso Robles $22

Full and chewy with notes of cassis, fig, plum, dark chocolate, vanilla, and fennel seed

Vina Robles Cabernet Sauvignon Estate, Paso Robles $26

Full, expressive, dry, and lightly gripping with notes of black currant, fig, black olive, and espresso

Cadaretta Cabernet Sauvignon, Columbia Valley $45

Full-bodied, lightly chewy, youthful, and ripe with notes of crème de cassis, black olive, sage, black licorice, and dark roast coffee

Silver Totem Cabernet Sauvignon Horse Heaven Hills, Columbia Valley $20

Lightly chewy and dry with notes of cassis, black licorice, spearmint, dark chocolate, cigar box, and cedar

Argentina

Achaval-Ferrer Cabernet Sauvignon, Mendoza $25

Full, chewy, and fresh with notes of plum, cassis, blueberry, cocoa powder, carob, vanilla bean, and mocha

El Esteco Cabernet Sauvignon, Calchaqui Valley $25

Supple, fresh, and dry with notes of cherry, cassis, blackberry, mocha, and vanilla

Catena Alta Cabernet Sauvignon, Mendoza $24

Elegant and lightly chewy with notes of cherry, cassis, black olive, dark chocolate, and clove

Susana Balbo Signature Cabernet Sauvignon, Valle de Uco, Mendoza $24

Full and chewy with notes of cassis, mulberry, leather, cedar, espresso, and vanilla

WORTH THE SPLURGE/SHOPPING $50 AND ABOVE

France

Château Batailley Grand Cru Classé, Pauillac $70

Complex, lightly gripping, and very dry with notes of black currant, fig, brown mushroom, stewed tomato, smoke, tar, and graphite

Lions de Batailley, Pauillac $50

Rich, dry, and gently chewy with notes of cherry, cassis, black olive, beef jerky, sage, espresso, and nutmeg

Château Calon-Ségur Grand Cru Classé, Saint-Estèphe $120

Firm, meaty, and powerful with notes of cassis, cigar box, tobacco, and seared steak

Château Cantemerle Grand Cru Classé, Haut-Médoc $56

Understated, subtle, and slightly chewy with notes of cassis, plum, mushroom, cigar box, and graphite

Château Langoa-Barton Grand Cru Classé, Saint-Julien $50

Subtly powerful and elegant with notes of tar, cassis, leather, smoke, and chestnut

Château de Pez, Saint-Estèphe $53

Finely gripping and fresh with notes of black cherry, cassis, plum, vanilla bean, and cedar

Italy

Sella & Mosca Marchese di Villamarina, Alghero, Sardinia $65

Velvety, chewy, dry, and tart with notes of strawberry, cherry, red licorice, black olive, fennel, and mushroom

USA

Château Montelena Cabernet Sauvignon, Napa Valley $58

Supple, balanced, fresh, and lightly chewy with notes of cassis, plum, black olive, and smoky vanilla bean

Jordan Cabernet Sauvignon, Alexander Valley, Sonoma $55

A lovely softer style with notes of cassis, black licorice, cedar, and mocha

Kenwood Vineyards Artist Series Cabernet Sauvignon, Sonoma $75

Rich and deeply fruity with notes of blackberry, black currant, Bing cherry, sage, bay leaf, menthol, vanilla, and tobacco

Maxville Cabernet Sauvignon, Napa Valley $65

Rich and chewy with notes of cassis, boysenberry, red rose, cedar, and caramel

Ridge Cabernet Sauvignon Estate, Santa Cruz Mountains $55

Very youthful and gripping with notes of raspberry, cassis, mint, maple, dark chocolate, and bay leaf

Robert Mondavi Winery Cabernet Sauvignon, Oakville, Napa Valley $55

Full, layered and initially plush, with notes of cherry, cassis, blueberry, fig, clove, and cinnamon, and a big ramp-up of chewiness—age or aerate

Shafer Vineyards One Point Five Cabernet Sauvignon, Stags' Leap District, Napa Valley $80

Powerful, layered, and balanced with notes of blackberry, boysenberry, cassis, black olive, aged balsamic, mocha, and toasted pecan

Sleeping Giant Cabernet Sauvignon Inglewood St. Helena, Napa Valley $80

Powerful and concentrated with notes of blueberry, cassis, mulberry, black olive, rose, dark chocolate, caramel, and clove; youthfully chewy

Silver Oak, Alexander Valley $70

Youthfully gripping and rich with notes of cherry, blueberry, spearmint, black olive, and coffee bean

Stag's Leap Wine Cellars Artemis Cabernet Sauvignon, Napa Valley $63

Full, plush, and rich with notes of cassis, rhubarb, vanilla, clove, and caramel chocolate

Stags' Leap Winery Cabernet Sauvignon, Napa Valley $60

Elegant with building grip and notes of black currant, black plum, bay leaf, cedar, and tobacco

Trione Cabernet Sauvignon Block Twenty One Alexander Valley $67

Warm and inviting with notes of cassis, plum, blackberry, chocolate chip cookie, mocha, and cedar; plush and full with a gentle chewiness

Pepper Bridge Cabernet Sauvignon, Walla Walla Valley $60

Rich, bright, full, and chewy with notes of raspberry, cassis, blueberry, dried bay leaf, and vanilla bean

CHÂTEAU LYNCH-BAGES—HARVEST OF 1993

One of my dreams, nurtured quietly during those unending winters in upper New York State's snow belt—Cornell University is in Ithaca—was to live in a tropical paradise. Hawaii seemed the logical choice, so when I left New York City, I moved to Oahu and began working part-time as a sommelier at the New Otani Kaimana Beach Hotel, and full time as wine manager for the state's largest distributor, Paradise Beverage. By that time, I had begun studying to become a Master Sommelier. I found a few colleagues to study and taste with, and completed the preliminary exams by early 1993.

I still had the dream of working the harvest in Europe, though. Being a pushy New Yorker, while not very useful for settling into island life, helped the cause, as I finally was able to convince Brigitte Plummer of Seagram Château & Estates to make the necessary arrangements. I was to work the *vendange*, or harvest, of 1993 with Jean-Michel Cazes and his sister Sylvie, as well as with the AXA technical director Daniel Llose at one or two of the AXA Insurance group properties, including Château Pichon-Longueville-Baron, and at the family-owned Château Lynch-Bages. I was to stay with the *stagiaires*—interns who stayed for several months to learn the tricks of the trade—and to work in the fields as well as in the *chai*, the cellar. I did expect, even embrace the hard work. But I didn't count on all the rain.

Instead of shopping for sunscreen and work gloves, I should've been shopping for an industrial-strength slicker and galoshes! The crush of 1993 was a wet one. The best properties in the Médoc are located along the riverbank with deep, well-draining, gravelly soil. Flooding was common in the lesser sites, the extra water bloating the grapes, leading to wines of less precise character.

What made the greatest impression on me during those two weeks was the spirit of the workers, many from northern Spain and Portugal. Despite the inclement weather, and the long days of backbreaking labor, these people were having fun! In fact, one day, they decided to inaugurate me, the silly American girl who was actually doing this for free, into the *équipe*, or team. Little by little, throughout that day, they would tease me by stuffing a bunch of grapes down the back of my boots, or into my turtleneck.

They became brasher as the day went on. I was called up to the *table de tries*, or sorting table. This was considered a promotion, because you got to stand upright, and you got to throw the reject bunches of grapes at the other workers in the field. You were no longer the target, or so I thought. I was impressed by the number of hands involved at all these preliminary levels of production. We may have been joking around but the work was carried out with the utmost of professionalism and with an eagle eye for quality. Picking grapes for a top Bordeaux house was something like putting together a Rolls-Royce. There were twelve of us there, sorting the grapes by hand as they came up off the backs of the pickers. This was a very labor-intensive business. No mechanical harvesters here.

By lunchtime, after several hours of labor in damp and chilly conditions, we had worked up a rip-roaring appetite. Aside from the deeply satisfying food, the body-warming fire, and the soul-warming camaraderie—singing and merrymaking were common—that day the divine Julia Child graced us with her presence. I recognized her immediately. I set down my glass of 1983 Château Lynch-Bages—yes, this is really what they served us—and gasped for air. What a thrill! By the time I had regained my composure, she had been whisked off to continue her tour of harvest luncheons.

Toward the end of that day, I noticed that the renegade grape clusters were going into my ears, down my back, and even into my mouth. I sensed that something was up—New Yorkers grow eyes in the back of their heads for day-to-day survival—but I didn't really care, because we were having so much fun. Well, they finally got me.

They hoisted my body up onto the sorting table, bombed me with grapes, and sent me, along with some suitable grapes, of course, into the vat of what was to become Château Lynch-Bages 1993. It was official. I was a member of the *équipe*.

DINING OUT

Since Cabernet Sauvignon is such an important, successful, and popular grape, likely there will be multiple choices even on the simplest of wine lists. Plug in your geography here to sift through the names. Look for Haut-Médoc or one of the village names. Ask for second wines, such as Château Batailley's Lions de Batailley, or Les Forts de Latour from Château Latour. (Château Latour is simply named after the tower— *la tour*—on the estate.) Second wines are produced from the estate's younger vines or lesser blends. They hint at the character of the first wines but are softer, more approachable, and far less pricey.

For New World selections, it is in restaurants that smaller producers, or those with a limited release, look to place their wines. For example, Terra Valentine, one of the best price-to-quality ratio Cabernet Sauvignons from Napa Valley, has a smaller production of a Spring Mountain estate release sold only to restaurants. Try this if you can find it: Terra Valentine Cabernet Sauvignon, Spring Mountain, Napa Valley $120 (estimated wine list price.)

BRANCH OUT

AGLIANICO

Aglianico ("ahl-yee-ah-nee-ko") is richer in chewy, mouth-gripping tannins than most Cabernet Sauvignons. The rules in Campania, Italy, where it is produced, require mandatory oak aging before release with the common goal of a softer, more approachable wine.

Mastroberardino Radici Taurasi, Campania $60

Savory, gripping, and fresh with notes of raspberry, black cherry, Brie, mushroom, foie gras, cedar, and nutmeg

This is the region's best. Let me know what you think.

Check Your Success Quiz
1. For someone just discovering red wines, would you recommend Merlot or Cabernet Sauvignon?
2. Cabernet Sauvignon loves the heat. True/False

10

ZINFANDEL

grape goddess says:
"Zin-fun-dell." Repeat after me: "Zin-fun-dell."
"Zin-fan-dell." Repeat after me: "Zin-fan-dell."

Go ahead, say it. Either way, Zinfandel is fun and will make a fan out of you. This warm, inviting, fruity, and supple red may whisper in your ear or shout from the rooftop, but two things are for sure: it will engage the senses and it will deliver pleasure. Zinfandel is a wine that makes people smile.

HISTORY

Many of the benchmark, standard, or point-of-reference wines, role models for the world at large, are in France. Pinot Noir producers look to red Burgundy; Cabernet Sauvignon producers look to Bordeaux; Syrah producers look to the northern Rhône. Zinfandel is the only major grape without an Old World role model. While European in origin, Zinfandel is the all-American grape. Why? The best Zinfandels in the world are produced in California. American Zinfandel is the benchmark for the world. Producers from around the world who are considering planting it look to those produced in California.

In the Middle Ages, a grape called Tribidrag was widely planted along the Dalmatian Coast in present-day Croatia. As Tribidrag mutated and adapted to local conditions, new versions grew there. One, transported to the USA, became known as Zinfandel. One transported to southern Italy became known as Primitivo. A version that stayed local was named Crljenak Kaštelanski, after the place it was found. This knowledge is all thanks to Dr. Carole Meredith's extensive research there and DNA testing here in the United States.

It is believed that in 1820 Zinfandel was one of several table grapes brought to the United States from Europe by the owner of a plant nursery. Immigrants in California planted it for wine during and even more so after the gold rush. Zinfandel was easy enough to grow, and the style of the wines they made was similar to that at home, especially for the Italians, who liked to drink it out of little tumblers, not fancy wine stems.

A century and a quarter later, it was dying out as tastes turned to Cabernet Sauvignon and Chardonnay. In the early 1980s, the Trinchero family accidentally "invented" White Zinfandel, which met with instant success. With demand for Zinfandel high, many priceless old vines were saved from extinction, partic-

Ten Grapes to Know

ularly in Lodi, a bucolic, rural area near Sacramento cooled by the Delta and home to growers of old-vine Zinfandel who would have gone out of business. Not only is White Zinfandel a friendly ambassador and wine-converting gateway, it is easy to enjoy, can handle spicy food or in-laws, and is available everywhere. Most notably, it is a strong economic engine for the American wine industry.

Lodi as a quality wine-producing region is only now coming out of the shadows, having provided so much old-vine Zin for so long to wineries in Napa Valley, and to the big names, such as Gallo. Lodi was the mistress. Trucks would come in from Napa, pick up fruit, and return with it via Lodi Lane. Lodi growers didn't have to rely on the whims of the consumer. It was easy money. Gallo grape-sourcing teams are in the fields on a regular basis to this day, communicating with and courting growers for their fruit. With top dollar being paid, did it matter if the fruit would end up in Gallo or other White Zins? Why not sell to Bogle, or Michael David Winery, who treat these growers like family and who produce old-vine-labeled Zins?

Single vineyard old-vine Zinfandel will never have the cachet of Cabernet Sauvignon. Even Zin-master Tegan

Lodi ZinFest

Lodi has more growers than winemakers. Its annual festival, ZinFest, celebrates the growers. Instead of black-tie auctions, these folks and some of us lucky members of the trade eat and drink, then throw off their shoes and dance under the moonlight. A few might sit back under the trees and smoke cigars while sipping on Zinfandel Port.

THE HAPPY ACCIDENT—WHITE ZINFANDEL

In 1972, Sutter Home winemaker Bob Trinchero let some juice out of his tank of Amador Country Zinfandel to concentrate it. What came out was pink and sweet. As a fan of French rosé, he fermented it and offered it in the tasting room. Since the fermentation had stopped before all of the grape sugar was converted to alcohol, the wine was slightly sweet. By the mid-1980s, Sutter Home White Zinfandel was one of America's most popular wines. Today one in five wine drinkers drinks White Zinfandel.

Passalacqua, winemaker for Turley Wine Cellars, the ultimate cult Zin, admits $38 is on the upper end for single-vineyard Lodi Zins. Lodi Native, a recent project focusing on the treasure trove of old-vine vineyards produced in a noninterventionist method—native yeast for fermentation and no new oak or additives—sells a six-pack for $180, or $30 per bottle.

Architected, under-$20 styles, such as The Seven Deadly Zins from the Michael David Winery, have been widely successful, bringing hundreds of thousands of new customers to the name Lodi and to Zinfandel. With lavishly ripe fruit, sweet oak, and a touch of sugar, this crowd-pleasing style inspired the new category of "dark" wines, such as Apothic Red. These dark-labeled, dark-named wines are so pleasantly sweet and eminently drinkable that they have cannibalized the Zin market even further. These days, grape prices are again falling for Zinfandel. Some growers are looking at ripping out their vines, and replacing them with Pinot Grigio, Malbec, or even esoteric Teroldego. This is a shame. Such organizations as ZAP—Zinfandel Advocates and Producers—hold annual events to help promote this underappreciated grape.

GEOGRAPHY

Zinfandel has a hearty nature, is adaptable to a wide range of soils and climates, and tends to produce a large crop. It ripens unevenly within the same cluster, causing a challenge at harvest time.

The best Zinfandels come from California's Mendocino, Sonoma's Dry Creek Valley and Russian River Valley, Napa Valley, Lodi, Amador County, and Paso Robles. In all but Paso Robles, there are 70- to 100-year-old vines, giving the depth of character and exquisite balance impossible to attain from young vines. A Heritage Vineyard is planted in Oakville, Napa Valley, to isolate these old vine clones and replicate them for new plantings.

Southern Italy's Puglia, with its significant port at Bari, is the only place in Italy growing Primitivo. Unlike other areas of Italy, Puglia is more flat than hilly. Its fertile plains produce wheat for pasta, olives for oil, and grapes for wine. Primitivo thrives near Bari, in Murgia, named after Murgese wild horses introduced during Spanish rule. Primitivo also thrives farther south near Salento, in Manduria. For a short time, Italian Primitivo producers were adding the name Zinfandel to the front label of wines shipped to the United States, and it worked. I remember seeing end stacks of Primitivo everywhere. But with DNA testing and label law, this is not happening anymore.

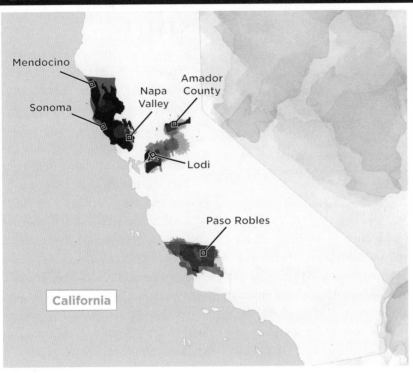

USA: California:

- Mendocino
- Sonoma: Dry Creek Valley, Russian River Valley
- Napa Valley
- Lodi
- Amador County
- Paso Robles

Italy: Puglia (Primitivo): Murgia, Manduria

TASTE PROFILE AND STYLES

Zinfandel is vibrantly fruity, with notes of raspberry, blackberry, blueberry, and boysenberry. Beyond fruit there are herbal, earth, meat, and spice notes as well as notes of vanilla, cedar, mocha or espresso, and cinnamon Red Hots from oak. Old-vine Zinfandels are the most complex and the most introverted. If you are interested, share a six-pack of Lodi Native with some friends, and then have one-on-one time with the gems from these cherished old plants. Without sugar and oak, they are the truest, greatest expressions of Zinfandel on the planet. If California had Grand Crus, these old-vine vineyards would be at the top of the list.

Aside from flavors, body ranges from light and sweet, as in White Zinfandel, to light and dry rosé of Zinfandel. The lightest red is the Claret style, "Claret" referring to an old, pale style of Bordeaux. Napa's Storybook Mountain is a classic producer of this restrained, elegant style. Easygoing under-$15 Zins, such as the Ravenswood Vintners Blend, are made in this lighter style as well, though there may be a touch of sweetness, From here the style gets richer, rounder, warmer, jammier, and spicier.

MUSICIAN

Kelly Clarkson is an all-American girl, a powerhouse with a soft, tender side. This soulful singer delivers the goods every time.

DATING PROFILE

- I am outgoing, exuberant, colorful, and fun.
- I am as down-to-earth as they come.
- I am always raring to go.
- I prefer dancing to shopping.
- Let's hang out under the moon and stars.
- Cigars? Sure, no problem. I can be sweet enough to handle them.

These hedonistic technicolor Zins dazzle and wow folks. It's as if they were ready for their Instagram moment. Alcohols range from 15.5 to as high as 17% ABV. The best maintain naturally high acids to balance their rich fruit and high alcohol levels. Zinfandel captures the spirit of the California lifestyle. Acid keeps things in check.

Turley Wine Cellars winemaker Tegan Passalacqua adds, "Lodi and Sicily have a lot in common. The resurgence is in wines that are transparent. Sicilian and Lodi wines have alcohol, acid, and color."

SENSE EXERCISE

Zinfandel Notes
This will require a few ingredients and at least one partner.
- Cinnamon Red Hots candy
- Vanilla ice cream
- Raspberry, blackberry, boysenberry, and/or blueberry jam
- Toasted white bread triangles
- Espresso or dark roast coffee

Lay out the ingredients on a table. Taste each component separately. Then, start to "compound" or layer them together, as in spreading jam on the toast and sipping the coffee. Just relax and enjoy the sensations. Later on, when tasting Zinfandel, you might be surprised how easily these descriptive words pop into your brain.

MATCHMAKING

With so much mouth-filling fruit, high alcohol, and oak, Zins are eminently enjoyable on their own. As the wines get richer and oakier, the less heat and spice they can handle. Otherwise, with their blessing of high natural acidity, these juicy reds are ready to rock the table. From the grill to desserts and cigars, Zin has it covered. Layne Montgomery, the co-owner and winemaker at m2 Wines, says, "What should I pair with this? A second bottle." Harney Lane matriarch Kathy Mettler says, "A bubble bath."

EVERY DAY WITH ZINFANDEL
Salmon
Lake trout
Halibut

Orange-glazed duck

Roast turkey

Beef Stroganoff

Red pepper oil crusted rib eye

Slow-braised beef

Roasted leg of lamb with rosemary

Wood-fired pizza with sausage and pepper

Zucchini, bell pepper, and eggplant skewers

Baked stuffed green peppers

CHEESE

Brie

Blue

SWEET

Raspberry brownie

Red velvet cake

Reese's Peanut Butter Cups (with the Sobon Estate Zinfandel Port)

INSTA DINNER

Lean Cuisine—Santa Fe–Style Rice & Beans

Healthy Choice—Korean-Inspired Beef Bowl

Takeout—enchiladas

UPSCALE CONVENIENCE

Plated—Spaghetti Nests with Italian Sausage, Broccoli, and Hot Cherry Peppers

SNACK

REUBEN SANDWICH WITH WHITE ZINFANDEL

Pick up some rye bread, corned beef, Thousand Island dressing, and sauerkraut if you like, assemble, and serve with the pleasantly sweet and juicy Gallo Family Vineyards White Zinfandel, California $4.

DINNER TONIGHT

GRILLED PORTOBELLO MUSHROOMS

Soak the mushroom caps in Zinfandel overnight. Brush with olive oil. Grill over charcoal. Serve with flank steak or quinoa, along with the soft, supple, and intense Sobon Estate Old Vine Zinfandel, Amador $16, or the full, silky, and sweet-tart The Seven Deadly Zins Old Vine Zinfandel, Lodi $16.

SHOPPING
EVERYDAY VALUE/SHOPPING UNDER $20

USA
Bogle Vineyards Zinfandel Old Vine, California $11

Supple, then very lightly chewy with dark berry, vanilla, roast carrot, roasted meat, cumin, and star anise notes

Gallo Family Vineyards White Zinfandel, California $4

Pleasantly sweet and juicy with notes of watermelon, strawberry, and lime Jell-O

Ravenswood Old Vine Zinfandel, Sonoma $19

Mellow and fresh with notes of blackberry, boysenberry, pink rose, cherry cola, and root beer

The Seven Deadly Zins Old Vine Zinfandel, Lodi $16

Full, silky, and sweet-tart with notes of raspberry, sour cherry, sun-dried tomato, green olive, red licorice, dark chocolate, and cinnamon

Sobon Estate Old Vine Zinfandel, Amador $16

Soft, supple, and intense with notes of cherry, fig, dark chocolate, vanilla, red licorice, and black pepper

Steele Zinfandel Old Vines Pacini Vineyard, Mendocino $19

Full, round, balanced, and fresh with notes of raspberry jam, cherry cola, chocolate-glazed doughnut, vanilla, and cinnamon

Sobon Late Harvest Zinfandel, Amador (375 ml) $12

Rich and dessert-sweet with notes of boysenberry jam, chocolate pudding, root beer, Swedish fish, and marshmallow crème

Italy
Botromagno Primitivo Murgia Rosso, Puglia $19

Rich, gently gripping, and dry with notes of raspberry, cherry, red licorice, vanilla, seared sausage, and Brazil nut

Villa Santera Leone de Castris Primitivo di Manduria, Puglia $18

Ripe, punchy, and lightly sweet with notes of dried cherry, fig, cedar, vanilla, and milk chocolate

IMPRESS YOUR GUESTS/SHOPPING $20-$50

USA

Peachy Canyon Rosé, Paso Robles $24
Full and juicy with notes of peach, strawberry, watermelon, and pink rose

Château Montelena Zinfandel Calistoga, Napa Valley $29
Silky, fresh, and dry with notes of cassis, mulberry, mint, fennel, lavender, bay leaf, red rose, and vanilla

Dry Creek Vineyard Zinfandel Heritage Vines, Sonoma $24
Ripe, full, supple, and inviting with notes of raspberry, strawberry, cherry cola, dark chocolate, dark roast coffee, and grilled sausage

Ravenswood Zinfandel Belloni, Russian River Valley $39
Intense, jammy, and dry with notes of blackberry, forest floor, moss, rose, cedar, vanilla, and nutmeg

Ravenswood Zinfandel Teldeschi, Dry Creek Valley $39
Full, ripe, fresh, and tart with notes of cranberry, cherry, blueberry, boysenberry, and cedar

Ridge Lytton Springs, Dry Creek Valley $40
Full, bold, and firm with notes of strawberry jam, oregano, vanilla, cinnamon, and clove (74% Zinfandel)

Ridge Zinfandel Pagani Ranch, Sonoma Valley $40
Intense, rich, and lightly chewy with notes of strawberry, cherry, sun-dried tomato, red licorice, moss, sage, vanilla, and cocoa

Steele Zinfandel Century Vines Catfish Vineyard, Mendocino $22
Silky, full, fresh, and vibrant with cherry cobbler, raspberry jam, fennel seed, thyme, lavender, and warm toasty oak

Fields Family Old Vine Zinfandel Family Vineyard, Lodi $28
Jammy, ripe, full, and fresh with notes of raspberry, strawberry, blueberry, vanilla, and sage

Harney Lane Old Vine Zinfandel Lizzy James, Lodi $36
Nearly port-like with sultry red raspberry, currant, cherry cola, red licorice, and vanilla notes

Ironstone Vineyards Zinfandel Rous Vineyard Reserve Ancient Vines, Lodi $35
Full, lightly chewy, and tart with notes of raspberry, cherry, blueberry, braised meat, nutmeg, and violet

Jessie's Grove Old Vine Zinfandel Westwind, Lodi $36
Complex and balanced with notes of cherry, blueberry, root beer, molasses, earth, and porcini dust

Klinker Brick Winery Zinfandel Old Ghost Old Vine, Lodi $37

Richly flavorful and unctuous with notes of raspberry, cherry, cinnamon Red Hots, and caramel apple

McCay Cellars Zinfandel Rous Vineyard, Lodi $32

Full, supple, tart, and dry with notes of raspberry, cherry, green and black olive, oregano, and lavender

St. Amant Zinfandel Old Vine Mohr-Fry Ranch, Lodi $18

Supple and fresh with layers of dried cranberry, orange peel, spearmint, chocolate-covered cherry, red licorice, mushroom, tarragon, roasted eggplant, Chinese five-spice, and prosciutto

Van Ruiten Family Zinfandel Old Vine, Lodi $20

Full, luscious, and silky with notes of peach, orange crème, raspberry, cherry, blackberry, fudge brownie, balsam, seared pork, brisket, sun-dried tomato, and dried Italian herbs

Eberle Zinfandel, Paso Robles $28

Opulent, bold, and very lightly chewy with notes of raspberry, cherry, white chocolate, vanilla bean, cedar, spearmint, and black licorice

Peachy Canyon Zinfandel Westside, Paso Robles $22

Rich, chewy, and gripping with notes of dark cherry, cherry cola, vanilla cupcake, and underlying cranberry tartness

Rosenblum Zinfandel Richard Sauret Reserve, Paso Robles $24

Brawny and intense with notes of hot cocoa, chocolate-covered cherry, raspberry, boysenberry, brown sugar, and maple

WORTH THE SPLURGE/SHOPPING $50 AND ABOVE

USA

Dutton Goldfield Zinfandel Morelli Lane, Russian River Valley $50

Rich, silky, layered, and jammy with boysenberry, blackberry, blueberry, chocolate frosting, root beer, mocha, and both savory and meaty notes

Martinelli Zinfandel Giuseppe & Luisa, Russian River Valley $58

Chewy, luscious, and rich with notes of raspberry, dark chocolate, and coffee bean

TURLEY WINE CELLARS

The ultimate Cult Zin, Turley Wine Cellars Zinfandels are mail list only, which is why I have not included them in the shopping guide. Despite their richness and concentration, they maintain a freshness and finesse, and oak is always in the background. All are from old-vine Zinfandel vineyards across the state. Despite their cult status, director of winemaking Tegan Passalacqua says, "Zin is not this wine that's up on a pedestal. People actually consume it. It's a grower's wine."

LODI NATIVE

A group of local winemakers inspired by sommelier-writer Randy Caparoso have looked to their cherished old-vine Zinfandel vineyards, many over 100 years old, to produce pure, unadulterated wines that showcase the personality of the land and grape plant vs. winemaker style and technique.

This collaborative project, known as Lodi Native, is focusing on old-vine, certified sustainable, heritage vineyards, many of which are multigenerational family-owned sites, including Wegat, Soucie, TruLux, Schmiedt Ranch, Noma Ranch, Century Block, and Marian's on the West Side and Stampede on the East Side. The six founding winemakers, Stuart Spencer of St. Amant, Ryan Sherman of Fields Family Wines, Tim Holdener of Macchia Wines, Michael McCay of McCay Cellars, Chad Joseph of Maley Brothers, and Layne Montgomery of m2 Wines, agreed to a strict, noninterventionist protocol beginning with native yeast fermentation and the use of no new oak. In other words, pure, unadulterated, exquisitely expressive old-vine Zinfandels so full of personality they can never become mainstream wines. This is the discovery of real treasure, Grand Cru American Zinfandel, pure, simple, unadorned, yet rich, complex, layered, and so beautifully balanced they glide across the palate like world champion tango dancers.

Upon first sniff, they may not be for everyone. There is something more here than superripe, squeaky clean, and hyperoaked, and something less. Think of Justin Bieber singing without auto-tune—he is vulnerable, fragile, real, more human than superhuman. Now, add to that a lifetime of experience—think: Aretha Franklin, Stevie Wonder, Keith Richards, or Nina Simone—and this is what you get with Lodi Native wines. Rich, layered, complex, evocative, and timeless.

While each of these wines is unique, as you can tell by my reviews

Ten Grapes to Know

that follow, they do share similarities. Lodi's West Side Zins are deeper, richer, with notes of blackberry, earth, tobacco, and herbs, whereas those from the East Side are more perfumed, racy with bright red fruits, and not as much intensity of structure. Overall the climate is more Mediterranean than Central Valley, as Lodi enjoys breezes off the San Joaquin River Delta. The West Side gets the breezes first. It is also sandwiched between two deep sea ports, to the north and south, and enjoys the insulating influence of these bodies of water.

Lodi Native Fields Family Zinfandel Stampede Vineyard, Lodi
Fresh, expressive, smooth, and juicy with notes of strawberry, cherry, plum, dried fig, canned plum tomato, and cedar
Lodi Native Fields Family Zinfandel Century Block, Lodi
Concentrated and ripe with notes of boysenberry, cherry cola, dark chocolate, grilled sausage, dried herbs, and tart sour cherry/watermelon on the finish
Lodi Native Macchia Wines Zinfandel Noma Ranch, Lodi
Punchy, intense, chewy, and complex with notes of peach skin, strawberry, boysenberry, raisin, cocoa powder, tar, cedar, and root beer
Lodi Native Macchia Wines Zinfandel Schmiedt Ranch, Lodi
Opulently ripe and jazzy with notes of cherry, blackberry, pumpkin puree, banana cream pie, zucchini bread, chocolate mint, and aged Sumatran coffee
Lodi Native Maley Brothers Zinfandel Wegat Vineyard, Lodi
Juicy, deep, lively, and luscious with notes of strawberry, raspberry, black currant, fig, raisin, dark chocolate, caramel, vanilla, and white flowers
Lodi Native McCay Cellars Zinfandel TruLux Vineyard, Lodi
Big, brawny, balanced, and inviting with notes of orange rind, cranberry, sour cherry, chocolate-covered raisin, cocoa powder, stewed and cured meats, and cedar
Lodi Native m2 Wines Zinfandel Soucie Vineyard, Lodi
Silky, round, plush, and long with notes of red berry, candied orange, watermelon, mango sorbet, mint tea, black tea, Airheads Rainbow Berry Sour, and s'mores
Lodi Native St. Amant Zinfandel Marian's Vineyard, Lodi
Intense, layered, plush, and sultry with notes of raspberry, blueberry, boysenberry, red and pink rose, peppermint tea, dark chocolate ganache, and orange sherbet

Lodi Native Zinfandels are sold as a set of six different single vineyard wines in a collectable original wooden case (OWC) for $180. Order online from the Lodi Wine & Visitors Center at lodiwine.com. You may also reach out directly to the wineries. If available, individual bottles are $35.

DINING OUT

Zinfandels are easier to order as they typically will be from California, so there is no need to recognize esoteric European villages. As with other grapes, ask for the smaller, artisanal producers. One of these is Rafanelli of Dry Creek Valley. If you see Rafanelli on the list, and are a fan of the plush, ripe, richly fruity, and oaky styles, give this it a try. Keep in mind, too, that certain areas excel at certain grapes. For example, Napa Valley excels at Cabernet Sauvignon, whereas Lodi excels at Zinfandel. Both produce both grapes. But they only "master" one.

BRANCH OUT

VALPOLICELLA

Valpolicella from the Veneto in northern Italy has an affinity with Zinfandel in that it is made in a variety of styles, from rosé to regular, to a slightly richer Ripasso and then to a very rich and dry Amarone style. It covers the full range just like Zinfandel, but with more red cherry and red licorice than berry patch and herbs and no obvious oak taste or grip. Even at its richest, it brings fresh natural acidity for balance and freshness. The main grape of Valpolicella is Corvina.

Pick the style you prefer, from lightest to richest:

Bertani Bertarose, Veneto $16
> *Subtle, delicate, mouthwatering, and dry with notes of strawberry, cantaloupe, pink rose, and sea spray*

Bertani, Valpolicella $16
> *Light, dry, chewy, and refreshing with notes of cherry, red rose, red licorice, grilled sausage, and mushroom*

Tedeschi Capitel San Rocco, Valpolicella Ripasso $24
> *Fresh, dry, full, and tart with notes of cranberry, cherry, raisin, chocolate, mushroom, and cedar*

Tedeschi, Amarone della Valpolicella $60
> *Rich, full, and supple with a fresh, tart finish and notes of cherry compote, fig, dark chocolate, black licorice, espresso, and cedar*

Allegrini, Amarone della Valpolicella Classico $70
> *Deeply flavored, silky, and fresh with notes of fresh cherry, licorice, fig, raisin, mushroom, and Brie*

Check Your Success Quiz
1. Zinfandel is considered an all-American grape. True/False
2. Why is White Zinfandel so important to the American wine industry?

ACKNOWLEDGMENTS

I am grateful to Kevin Zraly, who taught me how persistence pays off before and during my tenure at Windows on the World, and who is one of the only men I have worked with that was not in the least threatened by my being a smart, strong, independent woman.

Without Madeline Triffon, the first female Master Sommelier in the United States, who told me to "put the blinders on, race like a thoroughbred, and give it your best shot," I would not have finally succeeded in passing my exams.

I thank Gerard Basset, the most highly decorated wine industry professional in the world, for his class, humility, dedication, and sincere guidance.

To the wineries, importers, and public relations companies whose wines are featured in this book, I thank you for your support. I would like to give a special shout-out to David Strada of New Zealand Winegrowers USA, and Randy Caparoso and Stuart Spencer of the Lodi Wine Grape Commission.

I am grateful to my Planet Grape Wine Review panelists and contributors: Liz Granik, Rich Higgins, Fred Swan, Liz Thach, and Deborah Parker Wong, and to Aimee Cronin at Drync, our tech partner. Without my web master, Douglas Burrell, America's first female-led wine review platform would not be possible.

A sincere thank you to James Jayo of Sterling/Epicure for the introduction to Ann Treistman at The Countryman Press, and to my devoted editor, Aurora Bell, and the team there. I am grateful to my literary attorney, Jessica Kaye, for protecting my best interests.

Thank you to my friends and family for your support and patience, especially my sweet boy, who sat by my side many nights, weekends, and holidays as I worked on this.

May the pleasures of wine enrich your daily life.

CHECK YOUR SUCCESS QUIZ ANSWERS

1. PINOT GRIS/GRIGIO

1. Yes
2. Yes

2. SAUVIGNON BLANC

1. Zesty green/zingy
2. Refreshing

3. CHARDONNAY

1. False
2. True

4. VIOGNIER

1. False
2. C. Apricot

5. PINOT NOIR

1. Chardonnay
2. No

6. SANGIOVESE

1. No—very tart, slightly bitter
2. True

7. SYRAH/SHIRAZ

1. Yes
2. True

8. MERLOT

1. Pine
2. False

9. CABERNET SAUVIGNON

1. Merlot
2. True

10. ZINFANDEL

1. True
2. The success of White Zinfandel saved the vine from going extinct and is to this day a huge commercial success.

RESOURCES

FOR ENJOYING WINE
Crate and Barrel glassware
Wine Doctor Classic Wine Preserver
Private Preserve Wine Preservation Spray

FOR FURTHER EDUCATION
Tasting/Sense Exercise Notebook

BOOKS
The World Atlas of Wine by Hugh Johnson & Jancis Robinson (a good global
   reference with numerous maps)
Oz Clark Wine Atlas: Wines and Wine Regions of the World (this book includes
   the best topographical maps for wine studies. It is no longer in print, but
   widely available used)

WINE BLOGS
vinography.com
wineanorak.com/wineblog
lusciouslushes.com

OTHER RESOURCES
Wine Aroma Wheel, by Dr. Ann C. Noble (winearomawheel.com)

INDEX

A

Aglianico, 168
almonds, 113
Alois Lageder winery, 45

B

beach wine, 110
biodynamically farmed vineyards, 138
branch out
  Cabernet Sauvignon, 168
  Chardonnay, 75
  Merlot, 152
  Pinot Gris/Grigio, 44
  Pinot Noir, 107
  Sangiovese, 124
  Sauvignon Blanc, 60
  Syrah/Shiraz, 139
  Viognier, 87
  Zinfandel, 182
Burgundy wines, 105–6

C

Cabernet Sauvignon
  branch out, 168
  dining out, 167
  geography, 154–58
  at a glance, 157
  history, 154
  matchmaking, 159–160
  overview, 154
  shopping, 161–65
  success quiz, 168
  taste profile and styles, 158–59
Calera Wine Company, 86
California Chardonnay, 66, 74
California Sauvignon Blanc, 57
Champagne, 73
Chapoutier, Michel, 138
Chardonnay
  branch out, 75
  and cigars, 75
  as cocktail, 74

  dining out, 74
  geography, 62–63
  at a glance, 63
  history, 62
  matchmaking, 68–69
  overview, 62
  shopping, 69–73
  success quiz, 75
  taste profile and styles, 64–68
Château Lynch Bages - Harvest of 1993,
  166–67
cougar juice, 67

D

dining out
  Cabernet Sauvignon, 167
  Chardonnay, 74
  Merlot, 151–52
  Pinot Gris/Grigio, 44
  Pinot Noir, 103–5
  Sangiovese, 123–24
  Sauvignon Blanc, 59
  Syrah/Shiraz, 138
  Viognier, 85
  Zinfandel, 182
Domaine Georges Vernay, 79
Domaine Zind-Humbrect, Alsace, 43

F

Ferragamo shop, 124
French wine names, 73

G

Gamay, 107
geography
  Cabernet Sauvignon, 154–58
  Chardonnay, 62–63
  Merlot, 143–44
  Pinot Gris/Grigio, 35–36
  Pinot Noir, 90–93
  Sangiovese, 113–15
  Sauvignon Blanc, 48–49

geography (*continued*)
  Syrah/Shiraz, 129–130
  Viognier, 79–80
  Zinfandel, 172–73
grapes, 11–12
Grenache, 139
Grüner Veltliner, 60

H

history
  Cabernet Sauvignon, 154
  Chardonnay, 62
  Merlot, 142
  Pinot Gris/Grigio, 34
  Pinot Noir, 90
  Sangiovese, 112
  Sauvignon Blanc, 48
  Syrah/Shiraz, 128–29, 134
  Viognier, 78
  Zinfandel, 170–72

J

Jensen, Josh, 86

L

Lodi Native collaborative project,
    180–81
Lodi ZinFest, 171
Loire Valley Sauvignon Blanc, 58

M

Malbec, 152
malolactic conversion, 64
matchmaking
  Cabernet Sauvignon, 159–160
  Chardonnay, 68–69
  Merlot, 147–48
  Pinot Gris/Grigio, 38–39
  Pinot Noir, 95–96
  Sangiovese, 118–19
  Sauvignon Blanc, 52–53
  Syrah/Shiraz, 133
  Viognier, 81–82
  Zinfandel, 175–76
Merlot
  branch out, 152

dining out, 151–52
geography, 143–44
at a glance, 144
history, 142
matchmaking, 147–48
overview, 142
shopping, 148–151
success quiz, 152
taste profile and styles, 145–46
Moueix, Christian, 146–47

N

Nero d'Avola, 124
New Zealand Pinot Noir, 94

P

Péppoli, 123
Petite Sirah, 139
Pinot Blanc, 75
Pinot Gris/Grigio
  branch out, 44
  dining out, 44
  geography, 35–36
  at a glance, 35
  history, 34
  matchmaking, 38–39
  overview, 34
  shopping, 39–43
  success quiz, 45
  sweetness, 44
  taste profile and styles, 37–38
Pinot Noir
  branch out, 107
  dining out, 103–5
  geography, 90–93
  at a glance, 93
  history, 90
  matchmaking, 95–96
  overview, 90
  shopping, 97–102
  success quiz, 107
  taste profile and styles, 93–95
Pouilly-Fuissé vs. Pouilly-Fumé, 65

R

Riesling, 87

Rosé, 39, 108–10
Rutherford Bench, 36

S

Sangiovese
  branch out, 124
  dining out, 123–24
  geography, 113–15
  at a glance, 114
  history, 112
  matchmaking, 118–19
  overview, 112
  shopping, 120–22
  success quiz, 125
  taste profile and styles, 115–16
Santa Margherita Pinto Grigio, 43
Sauvignon Blanc
  branch out, 60
  dining out, 59
  geography, 48–49
  at a glance, 49
  history, 48
  matchmaking, 52–53
  overview, 48
  shopping, 53–58
  success quiz, 60
  taste profile and styles, 50–52
sense exercises
  apple varieties, 12
  astringence, 15
  blind tasting, 13, 85
  Chardonnay flavor spectrums, 68
  finish, 18
  isolating flavors, 159
  licorice, 116
  multidimensional learning, 145
  Old and New world Pinot Noir, 95
  palate, 37
  recognizing Sauvignon Blanc, 52
  spice cabinet, 132
  tannins, 15
  tasting wine, 15
  Zinfandel notes, 175
shopping
  Cabernet Sauvignon, 161–65
  Chardonnay, 69–73

Merlot, 148–151
Pinot Gris/Grigio, 39–43
Pinot Noir, 97–102
Sangiovese, 120–22
Sauvignon Blanc, 53–58
Syrah/Shiraz, 134–37
Viognier, 83–85
Zinfandel, 177–79
skin contact, 39
Soave, 44
Syrah/Shiraz
  branch out, 139
  dining out, 138
  geography, 129–130
  at a glance, 130
  history, 128–29, 134
  matchmaking, 133
  overview, 128
  shopping, 134–37
  success quiz, 139
  taste profile and styles, 131–32

T

taste profile and styles
  Cabernet Sauvignon, 158–59
  Chardonnay, 64–68
  Merlot, 145–46
  Pinot Gris/Grigio, 37–38
  Pinot Noir, 93–95
  Sangiovese, 115–16
  Sauvignon Blanc, 50–52
  Syrah/Shiraz, 131–32
  Viognier, 80–81
  Zinfandel, 174–75
Torrontés, 87
Turley Wine Cellars, 180
Tuscan wines, 117–19

V

Valpolicella, 182
Verdejo, 60
Villa Maria New Zealand, 98
Viognier
  branch out, 87
  dining out, 85
  geography, 79–80

Viognier (*continued*)
  at a glance, 80
  history, 78
  matchmaking, 81–82
  and oak, 83
  overview, 78
  shopping, 83–85
  success quiz, 87
  taste profile and styles, 80–81

W

white asparagus, 59
White Burgundy, 44
White Zinfandel, 171
wine
  aroma, 12–13
  astringence, 14
  body, 13–14
  describing, 16–17
  dining out, 24–29
  history, 10–11

how to taste, 17–18
overview, 12–15
pairing, 18–21
shopping, 21–23
storing, 23–24
tannins, 14
. *See also* 10 individual wines

Z

Zinfandel
  branch out, 182
  dining out, 182
  geography, 172–73
  gift giving, 174
  at a glance, 173
  history, 170–72
  matchmaking, 175–76
  overview, 170
  shopping, 177–79
  success quiz, 183
  taste profile and styles, 174–75

ABOUT THE AUTHOR

While studying hotel administration at Cornell University, Catherine Fallis set out to explore the service industry in Europe. She was inspired by every detail of what made the elaborate European hotels exceptional. It was during these travels that she first experienced wine not as an elite beverage but as something interesting and accessible, and she has maintained this approach to wine ever since.

After returning to Cornell, Fallis became chef's apprentice at Chef Alain Sailhac's famed Le Cirque Restaurant, and after graduation took a position with Leona Helmsley at the Helmsley Palace Hotel in New York City, where she managed the award-winning restaurant Villard House. While brainstorming different specialties she could implement into her service repertoire, Fallis came across an article about Kevin Zraly and his wine school, Windows on the World, and was inspired to focus on wine. Zraly became an important mentor, and after much persistence, he confirmed she was ready and named her wine school coordinator and cellar master. When she was first introduced to the Master Sommelier program after meeting Fred Dame, she took an immediate interest.

Fallis moved to Hawaii, where she met Master Sommelier Chuck Furuya, who encouraged her to join the local tasting group to continue her wine education. While working as a sommelier at a beachfront restaurant, a wine director at a wholesale beverage group, and part-time in a wine shop, she began pursuing the exclusive Court of Master Sommelier designation with passion. Her journey took her to California, where she worked as Los Angeles area manager for Seagram Classics, wine buyer at Beltramo's Wines & Spirits in Menlo Park, and later served as sommelier and wine director at Michael Mina's renowned restaurant Aqua in San Francisco.

In 1997, Fallis became the fifth woman in the world to earn the title of Master Sommelier. At the same time, she joined the Master of Wine program and is now a second year Master of Wine candidate. She earned the title of Advanced Certified Wine Professional (ACWP) from the Culinary Institute of America in 2009, where she was adjunct faculty for 11 years, and is the only person in the world to be both a Master Sommelier and an ACWP. In 2011, she became a French Wine Scholar and in 2012, a California Wine Appellation Specialist. In 2016, Fallis was inducted into Les Dames d'Escoffier International and joined the Board of the American Institute of Wine & Food. She is one of a handful of professional sabreuses in the world, capable of opening a bottle of Champagne with a sword in a dazzling theatrical performance.

Fallis is the co-creator of the *Portable Wine Tour*, contributing author for *Oz Clarke's Wine Atlas, Opus Vino, 1000 Great Wines for Everyday*, and *The Global Wine Encyclopedia*, and contributing editor/columnist for *Tasting Panel Magazine, SOMM Journal, Glass of Bubbly*, and *Prime Women*.

Fallis is the Master Sommelier at Planet Grape LLC, a wine consulting firm providing content, reviews, corporate and private tastings, restaurant wine program development, and speaking services. She created her alter ego, grape goddess, to help bring wine down-to-earth for consumers as well as those entering the wine industry.

Her diverse wine background as a salesperson, sommelier, distributor, and supplier helped Fallis become the well-rounded and thorough expert she is today. She understands all facets of the wine business, and is a frequent speaker, event host, educator, and consultant for corporations, consumers, and the wine trade. Fallis is a highly-sought-after wine expert and spokesperson for the wine industry, and has recently launched Planet Grape Wine Review, America's first female-led wine review platform.

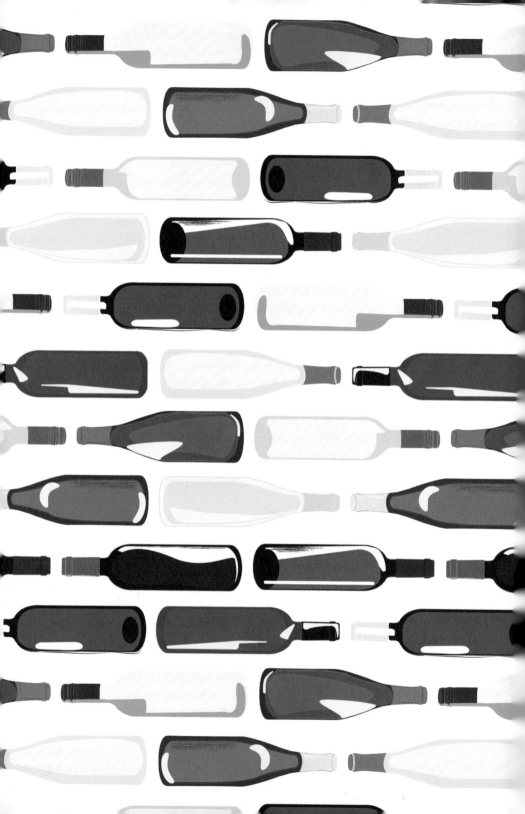